CW00434230

THE BERWYN MOUNTAINS

Walks
in and around the
Berwyn Mountains

John Tranter

First edition: 1999
New edition: 2007
Text © John Tranter

Copyright © by Llygad Gwalch 2007.
All rights reserved. No part of this publication
may be reproduced, stored in a retrieval system,
or transmitted in any form or by any means, electronic,
electrostatic, magnetic tape, mechanical, photocopying,
recording, or otherwise, without prior permission
of the authors of the works herein.

ISBN: 1-84524-089-8
978-1-84524-089-9

Cover design: Alan Jones

First published in 1999 by Gwasg Carreg Gwalch
12 Iard yr Orsaf, Llanrwst, Wales LL26 0EH
☎ 01492 642031   ▤ 01492 641502
✆ books@carreg-gwalch.co.uk   Web site: www.carreg-gwalch.co.uk

New edition published in 2007 by Llygad Gwalch,
Ysgubor Plas, Llwyndyrys, Pwllheli, Gwynedd LL53 6NG
☎ 01758 750432   ▤ 01758 750438
✆ gai@llygadgwalch.com   Web site: www.carreg-gwalch.co.uk

Acknowledgements

I am grateful to Margaret for her help in producing this manuscript and to all of the friends who tramped the Berwyn with me.

Walk Location Map

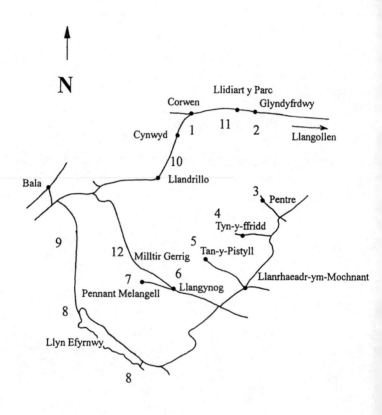

N

Llidiart y Parc
Corwen
Glyndyfrdwy
Cynwyd 1 11 2
Llangollen
10
Llandrillo
3 Pentre
Bala
4
Tyn-y-ffridd
5
9 12 Tan-y-Pistyll
Milltir Gerrig
6 Llanrhaeadr-ym-Mochnant
7 Llangynog
Pennant Melangell
8
Llyn Efyrnwy
8

Approx
5 km

Contents

Introduction

As you travel west from the plains of the English counties of Cheshire and Shropshire, the land soon begins to rise and the Welsh Mountains begin. The first major range are the Berwyn Mountains which are separated from the rest of the mountains in North Wales by the Dee Valley. They occupy a large area of land shared between Denbighshire and Powys and are bounded in the north and north west by the Dee valley, between Llandrillo and Llangollen, and in the east by the Welsh/English border. They extend almost to Llyn Tegid (Bala Lake) in the west, and reach down to Llyn Efyrnwy (Lake Vyrnwy) in the south. In the main they are quiet and lowly populated with a distinct air of remoteness, but there are many signs that the hills have been populated for a long time – possibly more than 4000 years. Most of the current population of the area is to be found in and around the A5 in towns such as Llangollen and Corwen. The towns in other parts of the Berwyn are very small. Despite the large amount of space and the fact that there are summits in excess of 800 metres, there is little tourist activity in the hinterland. This may be due, at least in part, to the fact that few roads penetrate the mountains and those that do are often single track with passing places. I believe that most people are unaware that the Berwyn Mountains even exist. Consequently, when walking in these mountains, there is a pleasant feel of solitude and, unlike many of our other upland areas, erosion is not yet a significant problem. However, many areas are boggy and peaty which means that damage can occur very quickly. Most of the towns and villages have a distinctly sleepy feel to them, and they appear to have been little affected by time. On the other hand, Llangollen is a busy town where there are always lots of things happening. However, there are no walks from Llangollen described in this guide, since the better walks from the town are to the north and west, and not in the Berwyn. The guide does describe walks that include many of the other towns and villages.

Geology

The Berwyn Range is a large upland area of Silurian flags and shales that were laid down about 400 million years ago. In fact this geological period, occurring at the end of the Lower Palaeozoic Era, was named after a Welsh Tribe called the Silures. Clay minerals (complex silicates containing a variety of metal ions) were deposited slowly into the deep Welsh Basin at a time when the north and south of the British mainland were separated from each other. The pressure of subsequent deposition formed the Silurian Shale which breaks easily in horizontal flat plates. It is not very strong and unsuitable for building purposes which explains the paucity of cliffs, a greater use of timber in buildings and a relatively small amount of stone walling in the area. However, low grade regional metamorphism (high pressure, relatively low temperature) has converted shale to slate in some areas. This can be cleaved into tough, waterproof, thin sheets and consequently there is much evidence of slate mining.

When the Silurian shales were laid down, this part of the world was in the southern hemisphere. As it slowly drifted northwards it moved across the equator and equatorial rain forests were abundant. The peat deposits in the Berwyn are a direct result of this activity.

The current shape of the Berwyn is the result of the last ice age cutting several valleys through the Silurian shale plateau and consequently, many of these valleys are the typical U shape resulting from glaciation. The higher valleys however, are often V shaped near the source of the rivers, and obviously the result of water erosion.

The plateau is typically around 400 or 500 metres. The major summits (Moel Sych, Cadair Berwyn and Cadair Bronwen), all in excess of 800 metres, are located towards the north of the region on a north south running ridge. They have a pronounced escarpment on the eastern side but other than this, apart from the valleys, the plateau is featureless. Consequently navigation is difficult when visibility is poor, and care must be taken in misty weather because you are unlikely to meet anyone to help you if you get lost. Added to this, paths which are obvious on maps are not always easy to find, or might not even exist.

Prehistory and History

This section concentrates on the visible effects that man has made on the landscape by his activities. Certainly he has been here for a very long time, and there is much evidence in the form of standing stones, cairns and stone circles, that there was a significant presence in the Berwyn from at least the late Stone Age or early Bronze Age.

There are two stone circles of interest in the area. The one at Moel Ty Uchaf (walk 10) is easily found and very attractive, consisting of an almost complete circle of about 12 metres diameter, of atypically closely spaced stones up to half a metre in height. The other, at Rhos y Beddau (walk 5), is more difficult to find because the stones are small and are hard to see in the ferns – consequently, winter or spring are the best times for a visit. An unusual feature for a stone circle in Wales is the remains of an avenue of stones running tangentially to the south side of the circle. Both circles have depressions in the centre, presumably for sepulchral purposes. If you venture to these circles in cold winter conditions, you will find them to be in most inhospitable places, both of them being well above the 400 metre contour. Our ancestors must have been much hardier, and/or the climate much milder.

Iron Age man left his mark on the countryside in the form of hill forts. There are several in the area, the most impressive being at Craig Rhiwarth (walk 6). The latter is in a superb position and was occupied from the Iron Age, through the Roman Occupation, to Medieval times.

The Romans came and went leaving little impression on the landscape except, inevitably, their roads (eg Ffordd Gam Elin, walk 10). Although most of Wales was occupied by them, in many areas – including the Berwyn – it was a military occupation where the local people (Celtic farmers) carried on more or less as before. This probably led to tribal cohesion which made it necessary for Offa to build his dyke, more for demarcation than defence, in the 8th century. This is not the only embankment to be found in the area: two others of a later age (probably late medieval) can be found near Llanrhaeadr ym Mochnant at GR133232 and 125218. However, like Offa's Dyke, they are not included in walks in this guide.

Wales was never conquered by William the Conqueror, and judging by the high concentration of Motte and Bailey Castles along the English/Welsh border, there must have been a great deal of conflict during that period. The remains of this type of castle are found in the Berwyn, usually in the valleys. Owain Glyndŵr's mount (walk 2) is probably one of them. Conflict between the English and the Welsh continued for several centuries: notable events in and around the Berwyn include Henry II's defeat by Owain Gwynedd (walks 1 and 3), and of course the exploits of one of the greatest of Welsh heroes, Owain Glyndŵr (walk 1). The latter, of mixed Anglo-Welsh ancestry, originally served in the court of the English king, Richard II. After the latter's death, there were hard times in Britain and the new king, Henry IV, unlike his predecessor, was not pro Welsh. This led to much conflict between England and Wales and for a time, Owain Glyndŵr was spectacularly successful in uniting the whole of Wales. He took the title Prince of Wales and defeated Henry IV in 1402. However, his success was short lived, and by 1406 the Welsh confidence began to fail. Glyndŵr and his son Maredudd continued guerrilla warfare but he disappeared in 1412. The revolt may have been over, but this may be regarded as the beginning of Welsh nationalism.

The Roman roads confined themselves mainly to the valleys; for example, what is now the A5 in the Dee Valley was a Roman road. However, of more interest and influence on the Berwyn are the Drovers' roads. From Norman times through to the middle of the last century, drovers would drive cattle from Anglesey and the Welsh coast to England for fattening and sale. The Berwyn Mountains were one of the barriers that had to be crossed. There are many ancient pathways in the Berwyn that will have been used by the drovers, and some are included on walk 3.

As with the prehistorical evidence, historical signs of man's endeavours are often spiritual in nature, since the area has some beautiful churches and chapels. Pride of place must go to the Church at Pennant Melangell (walk 7). The recently restored building is 12th century, but there is evidence of a much earlier building, and the whole site is on top of a Bronze Age settlement. Other places worthy of visits are the medieval Llangar Church, and the early 13^{th}C church of St Mael and St Sulien's in Corwen (walk 1). Also of significant note is the Chapel at Llanrhaeadr ym Mochnant since Bishop Morgan (1545-1604), who translated the bible into Welsh, was the vicar here.

Other historical relics are commercial in nature, with both lead and slate mining being widely spread across the area (walks 2 and 5).

Apart from forestry plantations, the largest sign of mans' industry is Llyn Efyrnwy (Lake Vyrnwy), its dam and its gothic tower (walk 8). Here the water from the Berwyn is collected for the population of Liverpool, almost 50 miles away to the north east.

Natural History

The flora and fauna is typical of that of other areas of upland Britain. Predatory birds are well represented and as well as regular sightings of buzzard, you may well see peregrine falcons, hen harriers and merlin. To the south of the region, there is also a chance that you may see red kite. Other moor land birds include meadow pipits, sky larks, wheatears, ring ouzel, red grouse and the occasional black grouse. For heather moors of the type found in the Berwyn Mountains, the numbers of red grouse appear low compared to similar upland areas in other parts of the Britain and, over recent years, the numbers have decreased dramatically in some areas.

As in many other areas, mammals, amphibians and reptiles are not always easy to find, but they are all represented here. On various walks I have seen foxes, hares, rabbits, squirrels, lizards, snakes and frogs.

The upland flora consists mainly of grass, heather, bilberry, cotton grass and ferns, but there are some rarities including cloudberry. For bryologists, the boggy nature of the area encourages a wide range of mosses and liverworts.

The Berwyn Nuttalls

A Nuttall is defined as a mountain of 2,000 feet (610 metres) or more with at least a 50 foot (15 metre) rise above its surroundings on all sides. Of the 181 such tops listed in Wales by John and Anne Nuttall in their book, "The Mountains of England and Wales, Volume 1, Wales", 24 are to be found in the Berwyn (see Appendix A) – a significant number. In fact, I believe there is a case for the inclusion of Moel y Cerrigduon (GR 923241) for, whilst it is nearer to some of the Aran tops to the west, it is in the same high ground as other Berwyn tops to the north. Also, it is east of the road through Cwm Cynllwyd, which may be considered to be a natural boundary between the Aran and the Berwyn mountains.

To complete all 24 mountains in one trip is a formidable challenge, involving a distance in excess of 50 kilometres and a height gain of around 2,500 metres – not to mention the tough Berwyn heather since there are no paths to all of the summits. A group of my colleagues have completed this expedition – it took a little over sixteen hours and three food stations were used *en route*. It was a particularly arduous effort, only for the very fit and, possibly, slightly deranged. consequently, in this guide I have included routes for completing the Berwyn Nuttalls in 2 outings – walks 11 and 12. These walks still present a significant challenge – the distances and ascents are not that great, but remember what happened to Henry II (see walk 1). For those really hardy souls who wish to complete the 24 Nuttalls in one trip, these two walks can be joined together – appendix B describes the link.

The Walks

Grading
The guide is designed to give the reader the opportunity to sample the very diverse nature of this area. It includes both long and short walks, and directions as to where to find areas of both natural and man made points of interest. Where practicable, options for shortening or lengthening the walks are given. There are 3 grades of walk in the guide, which approximately meet the following parameters:

Easy: up to 10 kilometres and up to 250 metres ascent
Moderate: up to 15 kilometres and up to 500 metres ascent
Strenuous: Over 15 kilometres and more than 500 metres of ascent

This is a subjective scale, and some might find the moderate to be easy and *vice versa*. However, in general the paths in the Berwyn are not as good as in many other areas, and this does make the walks more demanding. Knee deep heather is the equivalent of a steep hill, and the two together can be desperate. Also, the easy walks may contain some steep ascents, but they will be short.

Access and Maps
All of the walks in this guide are covered by the 1:50,000 Landranger Map 125, Bala and Lake Vyrnwy. However, it is probably much easier

to find your way if you use the 1:25,000 Pathfinder series maps, with the following four maps covering almost all of the region:

805 Corwen

825 Bala.

826 Llandrillo

846 Tanat Valley

Not all of the walks in the guide are on rights of way or permissive paths. Even where they are, there is no guarantee that they are either easy to find or to follow. In several incidences, for example, rights of way are barred by fences with no immediate means of crossing them. Obviously great care must be taken when crossing fences, to avoid both personal injury and damage to the fences. Where there are no rights of way or permissive paths, I have not encountered any access problems, though in truth, this may be because I have not met many people in this area. On one occasion I did meet someone erecting a new fence high up in the moors, and stopped to pass the time of day. I suggested that access might be a problem on the grouse moors, particularly in the shooting season. His very matter of fact response was "There's enough room here for all of us" and it was hard to disagree with this, since I had covered about ten kilometres on that fine Saturday morning and he was the first person that I had met. Nevertheless, common sense dictates that grouse moors should be avoided on or about the glorious 12th of August. Also consideration must be given to people's property and cultivated land in and around the valleys. Once you are up on the moors and high ground, I don't believe that anyone will be concerned about your being there if you behave in a responsible way.

Transport:

Public transport is not available for many of the walks and to make the most of the area, private transport is required. However, here is a selection of bus and train services, with an indication of frequency, that go to, or near, some of the walks' starting points:

Buses:

Arriva Cymru (01352 758657) Number 94 – Barmouth to Wrexham, about 5 journeys per day serving Llangollen, Glyndyfrdwy, Llidiart y

Parc, Corwen, Cynwyd and Llandrillo.

Tanat Valley Coaches (01691 780212) Number 60 – Oswestry to Llanarmon Dyffryn Ceiriog, about 2 journeys per day, serving Glyn Ceiriog (more services) and Llanarmon Dyffryn Ceiriog.

Bryn Melyn Motor Services (01978 860701) Number 64 – Llangollen to Glyn Ceiriog, about 6 journeys per day.

Tanat Valley Coaches (01691 780212)Number D79 – Oswestry to Llangynog (1 journey per day) and Llanrhaeadr-ym-Mochnant (2 journeys per day)

In general, Sunday service is lower.

Trains:

Llangollen Steam Railway (01978 860975) runs to Glyndyfrdwy and Carrog (Llidiart y Parc). There is a frequent service from May to October, but outside of this period the service is sporadic.

The guide also contains information about local facilities such as camp sites, general stores, public houses and restaurants.

The North West Moors and Cynwyd Forest from Llangar Church

OS Maps:	1:50,000 Landranger 125, Bala and Lake Vyrnwy.
	1:25,000 Pathfinder 805, Corwen and 826, Llandrillo (for a very short section)
Start and Finish:	Near Llangar Church
Access:	From Corwen, follow the A5 west and after a few hundred metres turn left onto the B4401 towards Bala for about 2 kilometres (1½ miles) where the minor road to Bryn Saint starts on your left.
	If you are dependent upon public transport, the walk can be started and finished in Corwen.
Parking:	There is a short stretch of minor road, alongside the B4401, which connects two minor roads coming in from the left where there is ample parking (GR 065423).
Grade:	Moderate, mostly on reasonable paths and tracks.
Height gain	About 450 metres
Facilities:	None at the start of the walk, but Cynwyd and Corwen – through which you pass – offer a range of facilities.
Overview:	This circular walk starts by following the river Dee to Cynwyd, continues through the Cynwyd forest and across high moor land, before dropping into Corwen. The walk is completed by following the road back to the starting point.

NB. The moors are used for grouse shooting and it is advisable to avoid them during the shooting season

Walk One - The North-West Moors and Cynwyd Forest from Llangar Church

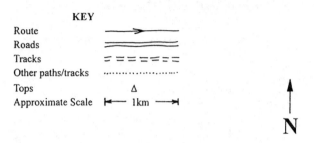

KEY

Route	
Roads	
Tracks	
Other paths/tracks	
Tops	Δ
Approximate Scale	⊢— 1km —⊣

N

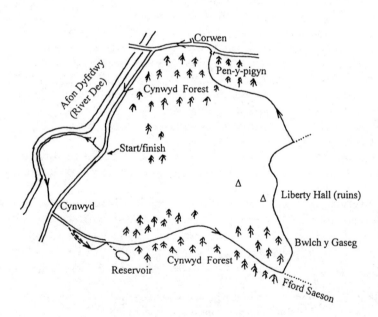

Corwen

Afon Dyfrdwy (River Dee)

Pen-y-pigyn

Cynwyd Forest

Start/finish

Δ

Δ Liberty Hall (ruins)

Cynwyd

Bwlch y Gaseg

Cynwyd Forest

Reservoir

Fford Saeson

Walk Directions:

1. Cross the road and follow the track North West (signed Llangar Church) towards the river. The church is reached by turning right, just past Stamp, after about 500 metres.

Llangar Church is beautifully situated in a peaceful churchyard with ancient yews and a jumble of gravestones. The interior has some recently restored wall paintings, but to see them you need to contact Rug Chapel. The latter itself is well worth a visit, and is located on the A494 one mile north west of Corwen.

Retrace your steps towards Stamp and turn right (north west) when you rejoin the main track. You soon cross a disused railway embankment and a field to join the river bank, and turn left. The river here, which is the Dee, is fast flowing on its way to the sea *via* Llangollen and Chester, amongst other places. Although the path is way marked, it is not always obvious, but just continue alongside the river. The flat fields with their lush feeding for the sheep and lambs, offer a distinct contrast to the Berwyn Moors. About 400 metres along the bank there are pillars in the river, which are remains of an old footbridge. The river bends south at this point, and shortly afterwards there is a ford, but you stay on this side of the Dee. After a further 400 metres you leave the river as it swings south west and soon re-cross the disused railway embankment. 300 metres further on, the path swings south east and becomes altogether more substantial.

For the next 100 metres or so the track, which was previously hard to find, has now become what appears to be a green lane. Each side is hedged and using the rule of thumb of one century for every different tree species, it must be around 500 years old.

2. At the road, turn right (south-west) and you are soon in Cynwyd.

Cynwyd is a pleasant little town with a variety of facilities including a Post Office and General Stores, two pubs, a fish and chip shop and the Barmouth to Wrexham bus also stops here. There are quite a few churches, a Youth Hostel and toilets.

Turn left (south east) by the Blue Lion in the town centre, and the day's climbing soon begins. After about 500 metres fork right through a gate along a track. Follow this track which reaches an old ruined building, surrounded by miscellaneous debris, after about 300 metres.

Go to the right of the ruined building and cross the small river (Afon Trystion) by a narrow footbridge.

There is an attractive waterfall directly in front of you, Rhaeadr Cynwyd; although not particularly high, it's quite vertical and certainly impressive. Looking back at the old building, you can see that although at the front there are curtains and it looks inhabited, several walls are missing at the rear!

You walk steeply up the right side of the falls and about halfway up you can get quite close to them and look, with care, over the falls. You continue alongside the falls until eventually you leave the mixed woodland, cross a stile and immediately turn left, back down to the river where you cross a footbridge. Follow the path and you reach the road after about 100 metres.

3. Turn right, and after about 150 metres you reach Cynwyd Forest. Take the left hand fork.

[The right hand fork goes to a reservoir inside 100 metres. This is a peaceful spot to take a picnic. You can continue along the river and eventually rejoin the original route, but it adds a lot of distance and some of the paths through the forest that are marked on the OS maps are missing.]

Continue through the forest with occasional large clearances, usually climbing but not too steeply, for about three kilometres. You are now on Ffordd Saeson (the Englishman's Road) and as you finally leave the forest it continues across the high moor land and passes to the south of Moel Fferna on its way to back to England.

Ffordd Saeson is probably called the Englishman's road because it was used by Henry II's 1165 expeditionary force during his retreat. His army had camped in the Berwyn Hills. He had been defeated by Owain Gwynedd's guerrilla tactics, ably assisted by the Welsh weather and the Berwyn heather.

As you leave the forest turn left for the last steep section to the highest part of this walk. For once, the sheep tracks through the heather go the way you want them to, and you reach the skyline at the north east corner of the forest near Bwlch y Gaseg after about 500 metres.

The views are now excellent and they are very open because there is no other high land near by. To the north you can see the Clwydian

Mountains stretching away to the horizon, Llantysilio mountain is to your north-east and Moel Fferna is to the east. From the latter the Berwyn ridge can be seen running south as far as Cadair Bronwen. To the north and east are extensive moors. Keep your eyes open for red grouse, the odd black grouse, and possibly even hen harriers. This is a very tranquil place and, certainly outside of the shooting season, you are unlikely to meet many people.

4. From the corner of the forest walk north-west on either of the two tracks heading that way. For the first 500 metres or so you go gently down and then start to gently climb again. The paths here are quite good and you pass the highest point of this area on the right (east) to the substantial ruins of Liberty Hall.

From here the views to the south and west now open up because the forest is not in your way. To the south-west, you can make out the south-western Berwyn summits on the horizon to the west you can see the mountains of Snowdonia stretching southwards towards the Rhinog Mountains.

Now you start your descent through the grouse moors still following reasonable tracks, until the north end of the Cynwyd forest is re-joined after about 2.5 kilometres. Follow the path down through the forest and in a little less than a kilometre, you reach a signed junction. The left hand branch is for Corwen, but take the right, signed to Pen-y-pigyn, and you quickly reach a large monument.

The large stone cairn, surmounted by a flag pole, commemorates the marriage of the Prince of Wales (later Edward VII) in 1863. It was restored by the inhabitants of Corwen to commemorate the investiture in Caernarfon Castle, of his nephew, Prince Edward, Prince of Wales in 1911. This is an excellent view point of the Dee Valley below and, straight across, of the Clwyd Valley stretching away to the north. It is a very steep drop to the town of Corwen below.

5. You now follow the signed path on your left to Corwen. This drops steeply through the woods. After a few hundred metres, you find a stone circle at the edge of the woods.

This stone circle has what appears to be a burial chamber in its centre but it is not of great antiquity. It is a gorsedd (Druids circle) that was built for the National Victory Eisteddfod that was held in Corwen in 1919.

Continue down the hill to the right of the circle and you reach the A5 in Corwen after a few hundred metres. Turn left along the high street and you soon reach the town centre.

Corwen was once an important staging post for the drovers, and was Owain Glyndŵr's head-quarters. Today it is a busy market town with several pubs, shops and churches. St Mael and St. Sulien's church, on your left and just past a modern statue of Owain Glyndŵr on your right, is in a pleasant churchyard as you walk through the town towards Bala. There has been a place of worship here since at least the time of the two Saints, that is around the sixth century, but the earliest stone buildings are probably twelfth century and most of the current building from the early thirteenth century. Over the south door is the famous cross-shaped mark reputedly made when, in a fit of rage, Owain Glyndŵr threw his dagger from Pen-y-pigyn. However, it is more likely that this is much older, and was probably the shaft of a Celtic cross which was later used as a lintel in the church.

Continue through the town and you will reach the river after one kilometre. Cross the bridge, with care since it has no footpath but carries a trunk road, and turn right across a stone stile into a field alongside the river.

From hereabouts, near a strange short wall made of large upended slate like slabs, you get a good view of the bridge which, whilst unremarkable from above, is most attractive from here. It is a six span eighteenth century bridge, and is listed as a building of architectural or historic interest. Stone built and looking decidedly worn, the shallow Dee rushes through it over a small weir.

6. Retrace your steps towards the town for a hundred metres or so, and then turn right on to the B4401. It's just over a kilometre along the road back to your car. There is no footpath but the traffic is usually light.

Moel Fferna from Glyndyfrdwy *via* the Nant y Pandy Tramway to the Deeside and Moel Fferna Quarries

OS Maps:	1:50,000 Landranger 125, Bala and Lake Vyrnwy. 1:25,000 Pathfinder 805, Corwen and 826, Llandrillo (the latter is only necessary if you plan to go beyond the Deeside Quarry).
Start and Finish:	Glyndyfrdwy
Access:	Glyndyfrdwy is a small village on the A5, approximately 9 kilometres west of Llangollen and 7.5 kilometres east of Corwen. There is a bus service from either Corwen or Llangollen; alternatively, there is a steam train service from Llangollen.
Parking:	There is limited parking at GR 149427 on the minor road (signed Rhewl) leading down to the railway station – otherwise, there is a large lay-by on the A5 approximately half a kilometre east of Glyndyfrdwy.
Grade:	Moderate, mostly on reasonable paths but there is a short section through knee deep heather. There are several options to make the walk shorter and easier.
Height gain	About 500 metres.
Facilities:	The village has a general stores/post office and a public house (the Sun Inn) which serves food. There are no facilities on the route.
Overview:	This is a circular walk which wends its way through the remains of slate mining in beautiful surroundings to the summit of Moel Fferna. The return is *via* grouse moors and Owain Glyndŵr's Mount.

Walk Two - Moel Fferna from Glyndyfrdwy

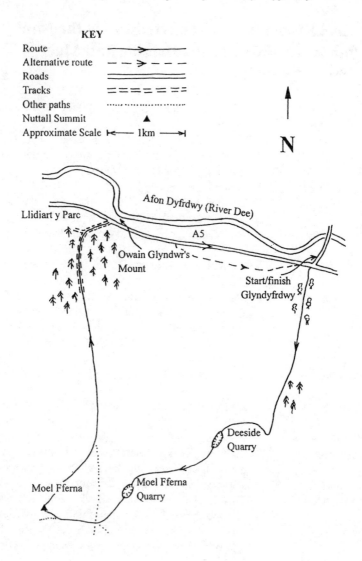

KEY

Route	
Alternative route	
Roads	
Tracks	
Other paths	
Nuttall Summit	▲
Approximate Scale	⊢— 1km —⊣

N

Afon Dyfrdwy (River Dee)

Llidiart y Parc

A5

Owain Glyndwr's
Mount

Start/finish
Glyndyfrdwy

Deeside
Quarry

Moel Fferna
Quarry

Moel Fferna

NB The moors are used for grouse shooting and it is advisable to avoid them during the shooting season

Walk Directions:

1. Leave the A5 at "Cofeb Owain Glyndŵr" – the village hall – (GR 148426), following the babbling brook on its left bank south along the way marked path signed Nant y Pandy Tramway. Follow the gently rising path through deciduous woodland past Tam Tympath, and cross the stream *via* a footbridge after about 400 metres at the attractive Pandy Cottages. Continue along the right bank of the steam for a further 500 metres, when you arrive at a small bridged weir and the first visible signs of the quarrying activities

Immediately above the weir there are many ruined buildings; these were the finishing sheds for the slate mined at the Deeside Quarry. Although ruined, the evidence of the skilled craftsmen is still visible in the well dressed slate from which the buildings were made. The works were powered by an enormous water wheel (no longer there), which was driven by water channelled to it from a reservoir higher up the valley. The slate that was mined in the hills at the Deeside and Moel Fferna quarries was transported to the railway station at Glyndyfrdwy by a tramway, which was almost 6 kilometres long and fell more than 350 metres. The carts were pulled to the top by horses, but free-wheeled down to the station and controlled by a quarry man on top operating the brake – a hazardous occupation which caused one death. The tramway was used until 1950.

2. At the weir, the walk now joins the course of the tramway up the valley. Soon after leaving the finishing works, there is a short section of tramway still clearly visible and some small waterfalls. The remains of the dam and reservoir which powered the water wheel at the finishing works is soon reached, and you now cross the stream by a slab bridge back to the left bank. About 250 metres from the finishing works you leave the woods, and the path joins a larger path coming in from the left near Nant. After another 500 metres you reach the old Tan y Graig mill, where the remains of the old water wheel can still be found.

[**Alternative short route:** at the weir, turn left across the bridge and follow the tramway course back to Glyndyfrdwy for a very easy walk of less than two kilometres]

Now that you have left the woods, the views begin to improve. In front of you is the Berwyn range with Moel Fferna on the right (south-west) of the skyline. The spoil heaps of the Moel Fferna Quarry are also visible, but those of the nearer Deeside Quarry are hidden from sight by a hillside. Behind you to the north, you begin to get good views of Llantysilio Mountain on the far side of the Dee Valley.

3. From the mill you continue along a good track up the valley, which turns sharply right after about 300 metres following the old tramway. The latter now gently rises around a hillside, and after about another 600 metres you reach the Deeside Quarry.

Although there are extensive spoil heaps, there are very few remains of buildings: this is because the slate that was quarried here was transported down to the finishing sheds in the valley for dressing. The slate was used for the manufacture of sinks, billiard tables, operating tables and gravestones. A compensation benefit for the workers, which they would not be anxious to claim in a hurry, was that they were entitled to a free headstone! Due to falling demand, this quarry and the finishing sheds below closed in 1923. The only occupants that you are likely to see around the quarry these days are ring ouzels and other mountain/moorland birds including, if you are lucky, a peregrine falcon.

4. Towards the end of the quarry, the tramway suddenly goes up quite steeply for about 250 metres to a ruined building – here it is good to take a rest and look back down the valley at the excellent views of Llantysilio Mountain across the Dee Valley. By now you have gained around 300 metres, but because of the constant interest and good paths, this has not been very noticeable. You now follow the course of the tramway west as it contours to Moel Fferna quarry, a little over a kilometre away. It is not always easy to follow the tramway because it is not regularly used as a footpath, and is often overgrown by ferns.

[**Alternative shorter route:** The Deeside Quarry is a convenient place to turn around for a shorter walk. Retrace your steps to Nant, but don't turn left into the woods. Continue on the main track for about another 200 metres, turn left and follow the track through the woods back to Glyndyfrdwy. Total distance is approximately seven kilometres]

There are far more ruined buildings at Moel Fferna quarry than in the Deeside Quarry. They are mostly located above the spoil heaps, since the slate that was quarried here was also finished here. The slate was used for roofing. The tramway was used to transport the slate until 1950, and then lorries were used until 1960 when the quarry finally closed.

5. Your route now goes very steeply up through the spoil heaps, passing remains of the tramway, ruined buildings, old bogies, hawsers and the like, to reach the ruined winding house above the quarry after about 200 metres.

One day whilst I was resting here and eating my lunch, I watched a fox hunt. There were four or five men, some armed with shot guns and walky talkies, and a pack of dogs. They were working from the spoil heaps below me across the valley away from me: the dogs appeared to be milling around fairly aimlessly. Occasionally they would get quite excited but I couldn't see anything. Suddenly, out of the corner of my eye, I saw the fox below me, running away from the hounds through the ruins between me and the hunters. I watched him until he disappeared, and it was obvious that the hounds did not have his scent because they continued to mill around across the valley. This pleased me because I'm always for the underdog or, in this case, the underfox. About ten minutes later, the hunters brought the dogs back to my side of the valley and I assumed that they would soon pick up the scent. However, this didn't happen – although they crossed his trail several times, and occasionally got excited, after about ten minutes, they were obviously going in the wrong direction: – Foxes: one, Hunters: nil.

6. Now you come to the hardest part of the walk! Until you reach a path going more-or-less east/west along the northern edge of the Berwyn plateau, there is no path. You go south-west for about 300 metres until you meet the path on the broad east ridge of Moel Fferna. There is only about 60 metres of ascent, but it feels like much more due to the knee deep heather.

When you reach the path, you get your first view of the main Berwyn summits – Cadair Bronwen, Cadair Berwyn and Moel Sych, which are joined by a more-or-less continuous steep east facing escarpment. The former is the nearest, and about six kilometres away to the south-west.

The scenery is typical upland Berwyn – a large heather clad plateau in excess of 400 metres altitude, with the main peaks around 800 metres high.

Heather clad moor land is typical of the Berwyn uplands and, in parts, there are red grouse. There is much evidence of grouse shooting to be seen, and this probably accounts for the fox hunt described previously since the fox can be a major predator of grouse.

7. You follow the path right (west) for about 600 metres (veering right, away from the fence, after about 400 metres) to reach the summit of Moel Fferna. There are two large shelters and numerous cairns but no longer the triangulation point which is marked on the map. Here you turn your back on the Berwyn and begin your descent on a narrow path along the broad north-east ridge of the mountain. After about 900 metres, you meet a major path running more or less north-south. You follow this left (north) leaving the long broad tongue that you have followed from the summit, reaching a large plantation after a further kilometre. The plantation is primarily coniferous, but as you descend further the number of deciduous trees increases, and it is a very pleasant woodland.

There is an abundance of pheasant in this woodland – presumably they are farmed nearby. The woods also contain other bird life including typical woodland species such as nuthatch and coal tits, as well as many squirrels.

8. You follow a major path north through the woods, bearing almost due east after 1200 metres, to leave the forest at the road (A5) opposite Owain Glyndŵr's mount. There are many major tracks through these woods – do not be tempted to venture east too soon because it is easy to loose your bearings.

Owain Glyndŵr's Mount is a 10 metre high truncated cone just north of the A5 as you leave the forest. It is said that he kept a look out for his enemies from here. This may be true, but the mount is much older and is probably the remains of a Norman motte and bailey castle.

9. You now follow the A5 for two and a half kilometres back to Glyndyfrdwy. You are now in the fertile Dee Valley, which is in stark contrast to the bleak tops of the Berwyn. It is a pleasant enough walk and you may see buzzards circling overhead, but you now have to put

up with the heavy traffic of a trunk road. It is possible to avoid the road and walk across the fields south of the road (*via* Carrog Uchaf and Allt-y-celyn) but this adds a further half kilometre or so, which is not always welcomed at the end of a long walk.

Drovers' Roads from Pentre

OS Maps:	1:50,000 Landranger 125, Bala and Lake Vyrnwy.
	1:25,000, Pathfinder 826, Llandrillo
Start and finish:	Pentre, near Llanarmon Dyffryn Ceiriog (Llanarmon DC).
Access:	From Chirk, follow the signs for Glyn Ceiriog and on to Llanarmon Dyffryn Ceiriog. Turn right, and follow the increasingly narrow road through Pentre to the very end.
Parking:	Parking is very limited here. At the end of the road (GR 130355) there is a turning circle (look out for the signs that indicate whether or not parking is permitted). If you are not able to park here, drive back towards Pentre and on the left hand side, immediately before the village of Pentre, there is a grass verge where two cars could park. From here, you can walk along the lane to the turning circle or, more pleasantly, take the track near to the church in the village in an easterly direction. Cross the river and turn left (north). After about 600 metres, the path re-crosses the river and you rejoin the lane about 300 metres from the turning circle.
Grade:	Moderate, mostly on good paths and, although sometimes the paths disappear, there is no real heavy going.
Height gain	About 400 metres.
Facilities:	None, though the West Arms Hotel in nearby Llanarmon DC provides excellent afternoon tea and scones.
Overview:	This circular walk across the moors utilises three ancient roads, and visits the Wayfarer's Memorial.

Walk Three - Drover's Roads from Pentre

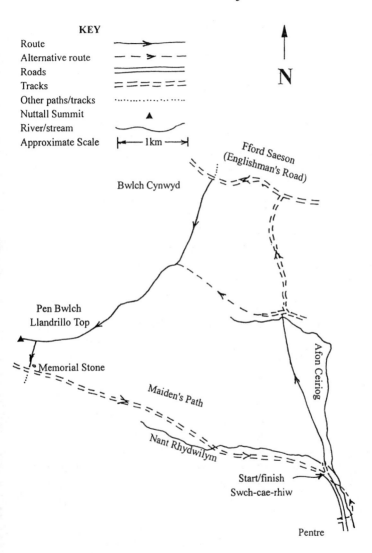

KEY

Route	
Alternative route	
Roads	
Tracks	
Other paths/tracks	
Nuttall Summit	▲
River/stream	
Approximate Scale	⊢—— 1km ——⊣

N

Fford Saeson
(Englishman's Road)

Bwlch Cynwyd

Pen Bwlch
Llandrillo Top

Memorial Stone

Maiden's Path

Afon Ceiriog

Nant Rhydwilym

Start/finish
Swch-cae-rhiw

Pentre

Walk Directions:

1. Turn right (north) at the turning circle, cross the stream (Nant Rhydwilym) and pass the solitary building at Swch-cae-rhiw. Very soon you will start to ascend an ancient track way once used by the drovers. After about 500 metres, the gradient begins to ease off, and you have done the hard climbing for the day. You continue heading just a little west of north across the moors, and as you do so the path gradually fades away. However, looking across the valley in front of you (through which the Ceiriog flows) you can see, going up the next hillside, a well defined track and the best plan is to aim for that. Although the path way is now hard to see, at some stage it was part of one of the roads used by drovers travelling from Corwen to Llanarmon D.C.

There are many ancient paths and roadways in and around the Berwyn – many of them not marked on maps, and often only short sections still exist. They may be observed as sunken lanes, green lanes, or merely scars across hillsides where the horizontal surface of the paths still exists, though they may not have been used for centuries. Undoubtedly, many of them would have been used by the drovers and although droving was primarily a summer activity, these routes would not always appear to be the best routes to the English markets. Often they involved crossing high and boggy ground. The use of valleys such as the Dee valley looks an easier option, but turnpikes were common on many roads and the drovers would be anxious to avoid this expense.

You continue across the moor keeping the high ground to your left, and eventually drop back down to the river (Afon Ceiriog). If you meet the river at the right place, you will find it fairly easy to cross. There is also an easy way of crossing the fence that confronts you. This fence follows one of the ancient district boundaries, and you will see some of the huge stones that were used for marking boundaries. These rough hewn stones were drilled to take strands of wire. The frequency of these stones appears to vary significantly, and individual stones are often marked on the OS maps.

[**Alternative shorter route:** Cross the river, and turn left (north-west) at the track which goes in the same direction as the boundary fence.

After a gentle ascent of about 1½ kilometres, you cross a fence and shortly rejoin the original route. This shortcut saves about three kilometres in distance, but little by way of ascent.]

2. Having crossed the river, a right of way is marked on the map across the moors in front of you, but this is particularly difficult to find in the heather and juniper. However, about 50 metres to the right (east) of the right of way, there is a track marked on the OS map and this is easy to find. You follow this, gently rising across the moor, and after about 1½ kilometres reach a T junction. This is the Englishman's road.

This is a very ancient road called Ffordd Saeson which means the English Man's road. It is so called because it is believed that Henry II retreated along this way after losing out to the guerrilla tactics of Owain Gwynedd, who was admirably assisted by the Berwyn heather and weather (see also walk 1).

3. You turn left (west) at this T junction and continue to climb very gently along Ffordd Saeson; after about a kilometre, you reach Bwlch Cynwyd. Moel Fferna is about half a kilometre to the north, and it would be easy to add it to this journey. However the route now turns left (south) and you climb gently up towards Cerrig Coediog. The path is quite reasonable, and follows closely the right hand side of the fence, passing many old drilled boundary stones. Like many other paths in the Berwyn, this one is often quite boggy – even in the summer. You follow the boundary fence, initially south, and then more westerly for the next 3 kilometres. The path does leave the fence for a short section after about 1½ kilometres, but shortly rejoins it (this is where the alternate short route also rejoins the main route). At the end of three kilometres, a little way past a stile in the fence on your left which you don't cross, you cross a fence to reach the small summit cairn of Pen Bwlch Llandrillo Top. This is the highest point of the walk at 621 metres, and it is the only Nuttall you visit today.

The best views of the day are to be had from here. Looking back north across the moors you can see Moel Fferna, with the Llantysilio Mountain beyond. To the west you can see the Snowdon Massif, and the Arenig, the Aran and the Rhinog ranges on the horizon. Cadair Bronwen is prominent to the south.

4. From here, it is all down hill. From the summit, you backtrack to the

fence, cross the stile (now on your right) and descend almost due south, reaching another ancient way in about 300 metres.

You have now reached the Maidens' Path. It is so called because the young women of Llandrillo would walk along this path into neighbouring Llanarmon DC to find work during the harvest season at one time. The drovers would also make use of this road. At the junction where you have joined it, there is a memorial stone, the Wayfarer's Memorial, to a well known cyclist and lover of Wales. There is also a log book, kept in a little metal box underneath a stone near the memorial, where people are invited to write comments. This makes interesting reading, though it is not in a very good condition. Opposite to the Memorial Stone, there is a sign giving access information for the main Berwyn summits to the south.

You now turn left (east), following the Maidens' Track gently down hill. You continue along this track for about four kilometres, until you reach the turning circle where you parked.

As you approach the end of this walk, the valley steepens and you can see the building at Swch-cae-rhiw away down on your left, towards the bottom of the valley. Nearby there is a small stand of Scots pine. Farms and inns who were prepared to welcome drovers and provide food and accommodation often indicated this by planting three Scots pines near to their establishments, and as a result there are many small stands of Scots Pines throughout the Berwyn – this small stand may be one of these. The last 400 metres or so of the walk is along a well defined green lane, and the number of species of trees in the hedgerow indicate considerable age.

The Cadair Berwyn Horshoe from Tyn-y-ffridd

OS Maps:	1:50,000 Landranger 125, Bala and Lake Vyrnwy.
	1:25,000 Pathfinder 826, Llandrillo.
Start and finish:	Tyn-y-ffridd
Access:	From Chirk, follow the signs for Glyn Ceiriog and then on to Llanarmon Dyffryn Ceiriog. Continue straight through Llanarmon Dyffryn Ceiriog towards Llanrhaeadr-ym-Mochnant, and follow the minor road for about 6 kilometres (4 miles) to Tyn-y-ffridd.
Parking:	Parking is very limited, but there is space for two or three cars near the stream at GR 119306. The best approach is to drive to the turning circle (where parking is discouraged) at the telephone box, where another minor road goes north to Maes farm. Turn round, and head back towards Llanarmon Dyffryn Ceiriog. After 50 metres, turn right (this is a difficult hairpin bend when approached from the other direction) and the stream is reached after about 200 metres.
Grade:	Strenuous
Height gain:	About 800 metres.
Facilities:	None, other than a phone box.
Overview:	A circular walk taking in the highest point on the main Berwyn Ridge and offering views of the only lake (Llyn Lluncaws) in the Berwyn Uplands. The Cadair Berwyn horseshoe is, arguably, one of the most scenic areas of the Berwyn Range.

Walk Four - The Cadair Berwyn Horseshoe from Tyn-y-ffridd

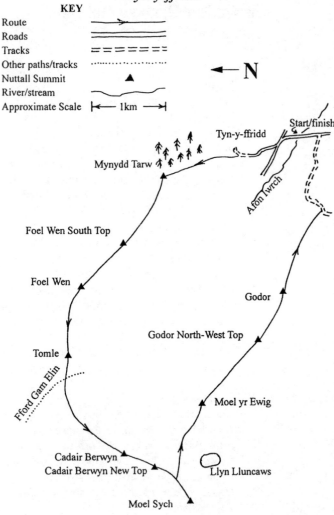

KEY

Route
Roads
Tracks
Other paths/tracks
Nuttall Summit
River/stream
Approximate Scale |← 1km →|

← N

Start/finish

Tyn-y-ffridd

Mynydd Tarw

Afon Twrch

Foel Wen South Top

Foel Wen

Godor

Godor North-West Top

Tomle

Fford Gam Elin

Moel yr Ewig

Cadair Berwyn
Cadair Berwyn New Top

Llyn Lluncaws

Moel Sych

Walk Directions:

1. Walk back up the lane to the phone box and turn right (north) along a minor road. Continue through Maes farm and after about 500 metres, where the track swings right, continue straight on (north) through a field. Although marked on the OS map as a right of way, there is no visible sign of a path, but at the far end of the field you meet what is obviously an ancient track. Follow this to the right until it meets the forest after a few hundred metres. The right of way now goes left (west), but your route continues alongside the forest, climbing quite steeply, for the next 800 metres or so to the summit of Mynydd Tarw. This summit is surmounted by a large shelter cairn.

2. Follow the faint path alongside a fence in a north-westerly direction along the northern limb of the horseshoe. The going is remarkably good for the Berwyn, and you reach Foel Wen South Top after about a kilometre, and Foel Wen in another 500 metres without any serious uphill gradients. Continue alongside the fence, which heads in a more westerly direction after a few hundred metres, to reach Tomle after a further 1.5 kilometres. The summit is marked by a small pile of quartz stones.

As you walk along this ridge, you get the best views of the eastern escarpment of the main Berwyn Ridge in front of you, and it is quite an impressive sight. From left to right you can see Moel Sych, Cadair Berwyn New Top and Cadair Berwyn. Next is Bwlch Maen Gwynedd which separates Cadair Bronwen, with its enormous summit cairn, from the main ridge. As you walk along this part of the horseshoe, it appears that the New Top is the highest point on the ridge and you wonder why this was not originally recognised as such, and was consequently regarded as the highest point in the Berwyn mountains. From some points on the main ridge, for example around the north end of the mountain, Cadair Berwyn does appears higher, but from most view points the New Top appears higher and measurement confirms this.

Continue west to meet the ancient track way Ffordd Gam Elin, after about 500 metres.

Ffordd Gam Elin is an ancient track, said to be Roman, which goes from just north of Llandrillo to Llanrhaeadr-ym-Mochnant, and crosses Bwlch Maen ˙Gwynedd, the pass between Cadair Berwyn and

Cadair Bronwen, which is about 300 metres to your right (north west). The track name means Helen's crooked road and Helen is believed to have been a Welsh princess who was married to a Roman Emperor. Just past the junction of the path and this track is a two metre long fallen stone, originally a prehistoric standing stone.

3. Ignore Ffordd Gam Elin, and continue west alongside a fence, climbing steeply for a few hundred metres to meet the main Berwyn Ridge. Turn left (south-west) and about a kilometre of gentle, though often boggy, climbing along the ridge will bring you to the trig point on the summit of Cadair Berwyn. Cadair Berwyn New Top, the highest point in the Berwyn at 830 metres, is a further 300 metres along the ridge, and is impressively crowned with a craggy outcrop. The col between Cadair Berwyn and Cadair Berwyn New Top is particularly boggy, and there is a large shelter cairn just before the summit of the latter.

The views from here are quite splendid. Towards the west, you can see many of the Welsh Mountains including the ranges of The Aran, Rhinog, Arenig and the Snowdon Massif. To the north, the Berwyn Ridge stretches away to Moel Fferna, beyond which you can see Llantysilio Mountain and the Clwydian Hills fading into the distance. Looking east from here, there is a grand view of Cwm Maen Gwynedd which you are walking around. The eastern escarpment drops very sharply to the valley floor, 200 metres below, and the minor Nuttalls along the sides of the horseshoe are clearly visible. In the distance you can see some English high ground. Down in the valley to the south, you can see the only lake (Llyn Lluncaws) of any significant size in the Berwyn uplands. Moel Sych is just west of south, and the south-western Berwyn Mountains fade away to the right of it.

4. From here it's a short walk south-westerly to the summit of Moel Sych. This summit is not aptly named (dry hill) since the approach can be very boggy. Retrace your steps to the col between Moel Sych and Cadair Berwyn New Top, where you will find a path to your right (east) dropping steeply down onto the south limb of the horseshoe. Sticking to the path alongside the fence you pass high ground (spot height 698 metres, GR 077319) on your left, which according to OS maps appears to be Moel yr Ewig. However, in their book, John and Anne Nuttall nominate a grassy summit (spot height 695 metres, GR

081318) as Moel yr Ewig, which is about 400 metres east. The latter is indisputably a Nuttall whereas the former is not, failing to have sufficient drop on all sides.

5. From here, continue south east over Godor North West Top after almost a kilometre and on towards Godor. The path is faint and boggy through the heather, but is recommended because the heather hereabouts is quite powerful. About midway between Godor and its North West Top you meet a fence, and the path alongside it takes you to Godor's summit. Beyond the summit, go through a gate and follow the right side of a fence, heading south-east, down towards the valley. Stick to the fence, although the path is not continuous, and you will reach a sheepfold in a little more than a kilometre. This involves crossing fences, and not always with the benefit of a gate or stile. Continue down hill, and after a further 500 metres you meet a right of way – a well made track with a hawthorn hedge. Turn left along this track, which takes a sharp right turn after about 300 metres, and joins a road in a further 700 metres. Turn left, and your car is reached in a few hundred metres.

Stone circle at Rhos y Beddau from Pistyll Rhaeadr

OS Maps:	1:50,000 Landranger 125, Bala and Lake Vyrnwy.
	1:25,000 Pathfinder 826, Llandrillo and 846, Tanat Valley.
Start and finish:	Tanypistyll
Access:	From the centre of Llanrhaeadr-ym-Mochnant, follow the minor single track road north-west (signed Waterfall Rhaeadr) on the north side of Afon Rhaeadr to the end – approximately 6 kilometres (4 miles).
Parking:	There are 2 small, free parking areas on the left hand side, about 100 metres from the end of the road; or there is a pay car park (modest charge) at the end of the road (GR 074295).
Grade:	Easy, but with a vigorous start.
Height gain:	About 250 metres.
Facilities:	There are toilets, a telephone and a small café at the beginning of the walk. The latter is not always open in the winter. There is also a small family campsite with limited facilities.
Overview:	A circular walk, starting at an impressive waterfall, passing a stone circle and returning via a disused lead mine.

This walk could be used as a basis for reaching the remote Nuttall, Post Gwyn, when the grade would become moderate; or even the main Berwyn summits (Cadair Bronwen, Cadair Berwyn and Moel Sych), when the grade would become strenuous.

Walk Directions:

1. Take the way marked 'path' just before the toilets in the pay car

Walk Five - Stone Circle at Rhos y Beddau from Pistyll Rhaeadr

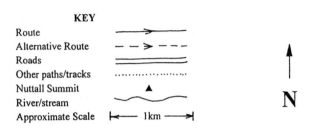

KEY

Route	
Alternative Route	
Roads	
Other paths/tracks	
Nuttall Summit	▲
River/stream	
Approximate Scale	⊢— 1km —⊣

N

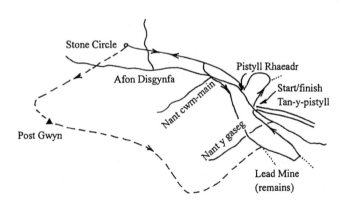

park. The path goes up through the trees, and you then turn left up a very steep zigzag hill. At the top of the steep climb, leave the main path and go down the gentle slope to your left through the woods, to reach the top of the falls.

Although there are excellent views down the valley, it is not easy to get a good view of the falls from this side. In fact, the best view of the falls is probably gained from the terrace outside the café at the base of the falls, where you can enjoy the view and share your scones with the chaffinches. If there is not too much water in the river, you can cross it just above the falls and take a cautious view of the water charging over the top of the fall. In geological terms these falls are very young, only having been formed during the last ice age.

2. Follow the north bank of this small river (Afon Disgynfa) through the woods, which is often boggy, until you re-join the original track shortly after leaving the woods. Now the walk continues up the gently sloping valley, keeping to the lower of the two tracks. After about a 1.5 kilometres, you reach a substantial ruined sheep fold where a stream, Nant y Cerrigduon, joins the river from the north. Cross this stream and, taking the right of the two tracks up a steep slope, you will arrive at the stone circle after about 250 metres.

This stone circle is made up of small stones and it is hard to find amongst the ferns and bracken in summer and autumn. It is about thirteen metres in diameter and an unusual feature, at least for Welsh sites, is a 50 metre avenue comprising of two rows of stones, running east to west which aim tangentially to the south side of the circle. These stones may not actually be related to the stone circle at all. There is a faint depression in the centre of the circle, which may be the remains of a burial cyst.

[**Alternative Longer Routes:** From this point you could head south west across the valley and climb the remote Nuttall, Post Gwyn. From the summit, you go in a south-easterly direction, rejoining the shorter route at Craig-y-Mwn. It is also possible to ascend Moel Sych via its western spur, but this is not as pleasant as the other routes to this summit – walks 4 and 10.]

3. You now retrace your steps for about 500 metres and after passing through a fence, you follow it down the slope to your right until you

meet the river. This is crossed wherever possible, dependent upon how much rain there has been recently. On the far bank, just over one hundred metres from the fence, you look for a path going south-east which starts where a stream (Nant Cwm-main) joins the river from the south. However, this path, like many in the Berwyn, although easily found on the OS map is faint and, certainly for the next few hundred metres, hard to find. You aim for the right hand side of the forest above the falls and eventually the path becomes more defined. As you leave the wood, the crags of Craig-y-Mwn come into view. These are the only real cliffs in the Berwyn, and not at all typical of the area. You continue up hill to the top of the crags and shortly after you cross a stream (Nant y Gaseg) that plunges over the cliffs, you pass through a gap in the fence.

The views of the valley from here below and arguably the most scenic in the Berwyn, especially if you walk 50 metres to your left onto a promontory high above the valley. From here, you get a good long range view of the falls, plus a view of the main Berwyn summits to the north. Almost 200 metres below on the valley floor towards the base of the falls, you can see two large pinnacles (Braich y Gawres and Braich y Cawr) which look most out of place in the green meadows. They are the result of glacial activity during the last ice age.

4. You now follow a faint precipitous path to your right (south-east) which cuts across the face of the slope, running steeply down to the valley floor. (The path is exposed and it can be avoided by staying on top of the crags for a few hundred metres, before turning left onto the main track back to the valley). After about 300 metres you reach the incline running down from the old lead mine, and if you follow the incline a further 50 metres down hill, you join the main path going back to Pistyll Rhaeadr alongside an old leat.

The leat, which carried water from the falls, was used for the lead mining operations. Lead was mined here from Roman times until the end of the last century. Despite not being used for a hundred years, the hillside has still not recovered and is littered with spoil material. Should you feel inclined to investigate the workings you will almost certainly be disappointed. It is a very steep climb with 100 metres or more of ascent, and reveals nothing more than spoil from the mine. At the bottom of the incline there are a few more remains of the mining

43

operation, and the wall of the leat is clearly visible.

5. From the bottom of the incline you follow the path alongside the leat north-west back towards the falls. After 300 metres you join a wood and walk along the edge, where you see the two very strange rock pinnacles mentioned earlier (Braich y Gawres and Braich y Cawr) in the fields on your right. There is now a choice of routes. Either follow way marked paths across the fields, which bring you to the road near to the car park; or more scenically, continue along the course of the leat to the falls, where there is a small bridge crossing the river directly below the falls near to the café.

Craig Rhiwarth Hill Fort from Llangynog

OS Maps:	1:50,000 Landranger 125, Bala and Lake Vyrnwy.
	1:25,000 Pathfinder 846, Tanat Valley.
Start and finish:	Llangynog
Access:	Llangynog is a small village on the B 4391 in the Tanat valley. It is approximately 19 kilometres (12 miles) south east of Bala, and 27 kilometres (17 miles) west of Owestry.
Parking:	There is a car park with toilets in the village next to the New Inn (GR 054262).
Grade:	Moderate, mostly on reasonable paths but there is a short section where there is no path. The latter can be hard to negotiate in mid summer due to the prolific growth of ferns.
Height gain	About 400 metres.
Facilities:	The village has a café (opposite the car park – a good place to start the day with bacon sandwiches and a cup of tea), and two public houses which serve food; there is also a caravan site. There are no facilities on the route.
Overview:	This circular walk goes counter clockwise around the crag, and includes visits to the fort and Bedd Crynddyn.

Walk Directions:

1. Turn right from the car park, cross the bridge and leave the B 4391 to join the minor road going north. At the T junction, turn right (east) and follow the single track road with the crag on your left.

Craig Rhiwarth, which dominates the northern side of the Tanat Valley at Llangynog, now rears steeply up on your left. A direct ascent via the scree and crags would be a desperate affair, and the defensive properties of the crag are very evident. There is a vertical ascent, in

Walk Six - Craig Rhiwarth Hill Fort from Llangynog

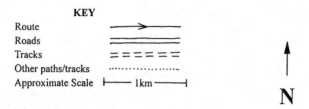

KEY

Route	
Roads	
Tracks	
Other paths/tracks	
Approximate Scale	1km

N

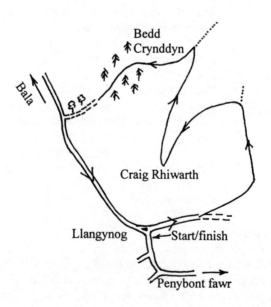

Bedd
Crynddyn

Bala

Craig Rhiwarth

Llangynog

Start/finish

Penybont fawr

excess of 300 metres, in a very short horizontal distance. If you look closely at the hillside you can see remains of mining operations that seem to have happened on almost every hill in the area at some stage.

After about 500 metres, you leave the track *via* a way marked path on the left, which angles across the lower slopes of the crags at any easy gradient. After a short distance you cut through the top edge of a deciduous wood, and after a further 200 metres you reach a stream (Nant Sebon) going more or less north-south up a valley.

2.   The path now follows the stream north and continues to gently climb, with the crags still on your left. After about 600 metres, take the left branch of the path and within a further 100 metres you meet a minor stream (near some sheep pens), flowing east-west. The streams actually meet about 100 metres to your right. You now turn left (west) and follow the course of the stream. There is no real path, just a few sheep tracks, and the gradient begins to increase significantly; a reminder of the good defensive properties of the crag.

This section is a real challenge in mid summer because, near the stream and the lower parts of the crag, ferns are rampant. One August afternoon, walking the route in reverse, I was descending with a group of friends into the valley from Craig Rhiwarth. As the bilberries gave way to ferns, it wasn't too bad initially but as we descended further, the ferns were taller and the footing less certain. By the time we reached the stream, the ferns were often shoulder height. As we followed the bank of the stream down towards the sheep pens it became very boggy, and occasionally we were calf deep in hidden streams and our eye level was way below the tops of the ferns. We soon learned to avoid areas where the ferns thinned out because that was a sure indicator of boggy ground. We were relieved to find the sheep pens and a good path, and decided not to use this route again in mid summer.

3. After about 500 metres, the slope begins to ease and you turn left (south) up a gentler slope towards the summit. The north wall of the fort soon comes into view, and you cross it to reach the highest point of the crag after about 200 metres.

There are excellent views of the Berwyn Mountains from here. There is high ground in every direction, with Moel Sych clearly visible to the north. The Tanat valley below us to the south is clearly the result of glaciation – wide and flat bottomed with steep sides. The fort occupies a large area, and is about 800 metres across at its widest. It was apparently occupied from the Iron Age through to Medieval Times. There are many stones in the area but an eye of faith (or great experience) is required to recognise the remains of the circular (older) and rectangular (more recent) dwellings, which are located more or less centrally within the fort, near the high ground. It is easy to see why they remain uncounted! The placement of the boundary wall however is unambiguous, and it must have been an impressive structure; it is still wide, but rarely more than a metre or so in height. It is continuous along the northern boundary of the fort and, unlike the hut remains, there is no way in which these stones can be due to the random placement of nature. The fort was only walled to the north and a short section to the west, because the terrain provided sufficient deterrent to the other approaches.

4. From the highest point you head more or less due north back across the wall, until you join a minor path which keeps to the left of the north to south running fence, which you meet after a few hundred metres. You cross a fence via a small stile, and on your left there is a young coniferous plantation which is not marked on OS maps. The path starts to go up hill, and you soon join a major track.

Around about here, you see several signs and a flag post – if there is a red flag flying, duck because, as the notices inform you, someone might be shooting. In fact, the rest of the route has much evidence of shooting and if the red flag is flying, it is best to go back the way you came. If it is not flying . . ..

5. Turn sharp left (south-west) where you meet the main path, and very shortly you reach Bedd Crynddyn – a large untidy pile of huge stones. I don't know who Crynddyn was, but he or she was obviously of some importance. It's all downhill now and after about 800 metres, the young coniferous plantation gives way to a mature deciduous wood (which is marked on the OS maps), through which a babbling brook flows. After a further 300 metres you join the road (B4391) which you follow downhill (left, south-east) back to the car park in 1500 metres.

Cwm Pennant and Santes Melangell's Church

OS Maps:	1:50,000 Landranger 125, Bala and Lake Vyrnwy.
	1:25,000 Pathfinder 846, Tanat Valley.
Start and finish:	Pennant Melangell
Access:	Pennant Melangell is reached by following a narrow road westerly for approximately three kilometres (two miles) from Llangynog (see walk 6).
Parking:	There is a small car park next to the church (GR 024265).
Grade:	Moderate, with a short pathless section.
Height gain	About 400 metres.
Facilities:	None other than a small gift shop in the church.
Overview:	This circular walk climbs out of the valley past an attractive waterfall, and up onto the Berwyn plateau.

This walk starts at a truly magical place in beautiful surroundings. Santes Melangell's church is about 800 years old, and contains a shrine to Santes Melangell. This shrine, reconstructed in 1991, is the oldest known in northern Europe, and is visited by thousands of pilgrims each year. At the end of the church, there is a reconstruction on 12th century foundations, containing what is thought to be the 8th century grave slab of Santes Melangell. The church contains many other gems. In the church yard there are several beautiful yew trees of great age – possibly 2000 years old. Although very few people live in the area today, the site has been occupied for many centuries, and the church is built on a Bronze Age settlement. Just to visit this church, which is open daily and has a small gift shop, is worth the journey. A few years ago it was in serious disrepair, but has recently been restored. The restoration is excellent and the building has a timbered belfry, typical of an area with poor stone.

Walk Seven - Cwm Pennant and Saint Melangell's Church

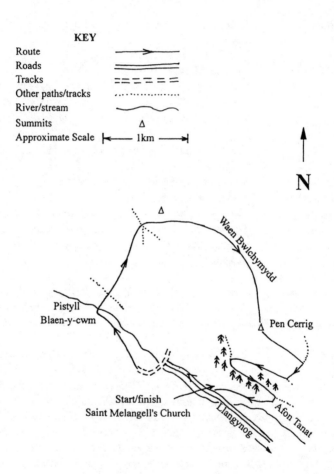

KEY

Route
Roads
Tracks
Other paths/tracks
River/stream
Summits   Δ
Approximate Scale |——— 1km ———|

N

Δ

Waen Bwlchymydd

Pistyll
Blaen-y-cwm

Δ Pen Cerrig

Start/finish
Saint Melangell's Church

Llangynog

Afon Tanat

Walk Directions:

1. From the car park, continue north-west along the lane. After almost one kilometre, turn left across a bridge and follow the track which soon bears right and reaches the base of the waterfall, Pistyll Blaen-y-cwm, in about 1400 metres. This track, obviously of great age, begins to fade and is virtually non existent by the time you reach the falls.

The waterfalls, again unsung gems of the Berwyn, are very attractive, falling very quickly through 100 metres in a few large steps. It is a beautiful and peaceful place to take a picnic.

2. Cross the stream wherever convenient, about 50 metres below the falls. Head north up the other side of the valley, to the right of a minor stream. There is no path here, just the odd sheep track, but fortunately there is no heather and the going is quite easy – except that it is very steep. By the time you reach an ancient track running north-west near the top of the valley, you have gained about 160 metres in a little over 250 metres distance. You cross the track, and head up north-east onto the moor. The going now gets tougher as the billberries are replaced by heather. Cross two fences at convenient gates, and you reach the main east-west boundary fence about 700 metres from the track.

The scenery is now very different from that in the valley. To the north, the heather clad moor stretches away towards the main bulk of the Berwyn. Moel Sych is prominent, and Post Gwyn is easily found. At 540 metres high, this can be a very desolate place, and you have now seen the full gamut of Berwyn scenery.

3. Head right (east) along the boundary fence, which follows the ridge. The going is reasonable, though sometimes boggy. After a kilometre or so, Cwm Rhiwarth comes into view on your left, and you reach Pen Cerrig (495 metres) after two and a half kilometres.

From here there are good views south-west, down into Cwm Pennant. Moel Dimoel, due south across the valley, is very striking, since it is extraordinarily steep near its summit. To the west is Craig Rhiwarth (see walk 6), which does not look as challenging as when close up.

4. From Pen Cerrig you descend south-east along the ridge, still pathless, for about 500 metres to a low point. Here you meet a right of way across the ridge, but it is not easy to find and obviously not much used. You turn right, south-west, back down into Cwm Pennant. After

about 400 metres you reach a forest and turn right, north-west, contouring across the hillside, and keeping the forest on your left. After 700 metres you reach a sheepfold on the forest edge, and turn left (south) on to a track alongside the forest. The track soon swings south-east and you follow it down through the forest, reaching some buildings at Llechwedd-y-garth after about one kilometre. Turn right through the buildings and after about twenty metres, right again heading west to reach the car park at Pennant Melangell in less than a kilometre.

[**Alternative Longer Walk:** This walk can be started and finished from the car park (GR 054262) in Llangynog. Pennant Melangell is reached by turning left out of the car park and following the minor road (1st right) for just over three kilometres. There are several paths to the right (north) of the road, but these are often hard to find, particularly in the summer when they are overgrown, and it is easy to get lost. Allied to the fact that many of the tracks are marked Private, No Access, it is probably best to stay on the minor road, which fortunately has very little traffic. From Pennant Melangell follow the original route to the low point below Pen Cerrig. Here you turn left, north-east, and cross the fence (no stile). There are only animal tracks here, but suddenly you come to an ancient track heading north, and down into the valley. Although obviously not much used today, it must have seen a lot of traffic at some stage because there is significant erosion. At the far side of a small wood, about 400 metres down the track, you reach a stream. There is a right of way on the near side of this stream, going north-east down to the road, but it is hard to find. Every now and then you find a stile with a yellow arrow to assure you that you are on the right track. At the road, you turn right and you can follow this road for about two and a half kilometres back to Llangynog. Alternatively, after 500 metres, pick up the footpath by entering Glanyrafon and crossing the footbridge. Follow it across the valley to join the B4391 near Tanyffordd. Llangynog is about 1200 metres down the road. This adds approximately six kilometres distance, but negligible climbing to the walk.]

Lake Vyrnwy – two easy walks

OS Maps:	1:50,000 Landranger 125, Bala and Lake Vyrnwy
Start:	Rhiwargor car park.
Access:	No public transport. May be reached from Bala on very minor roads, or the B4393 from Llanwddyn about 10 kilometres south-west of Penybontfawr, on the B4391 Llanynog to Llanwddyn road.
Parking:	Rhiwargor car park (GR 964242) and the Village car park (GR 017190) for the second walk
Grade:	Easy, but can be extended to moderate.
Height gain	Minimal on the first walk; about 100 metres on the second walk.
Facilities:	A visitors notice board and picnic area are located near the Rhiwargor car park. There are a variety of facilities near the Village car park, including a Tourist Information Office, an RSPB shop, Visitor Centre, Craft Shops and a cafe.
Overview*:*	Two easy walks, next to a lake in a beautiful valley, with lots of bird life based on the Rhiwargor, Water and Craig Garth - Bwlch trails, which are easily joined by a short car journey. Leaflets for these trails may be obtained at the Tourist Information Office.

Walk Directions:

1. After sharing your snack with the chaffinches in the picnic area, follow the way mark path north-west through the picnic area to the river (Afon Eiddew). Stay on the south bank of the river and continue west, with occasional glimpses of the waterfall. For a close view of the waterfall, ignore any way marks and continue on the south bank. You reach the base of the falls about one kilometre from the car park.

Walk Eight - Lake Vyrnwy: two easy walks

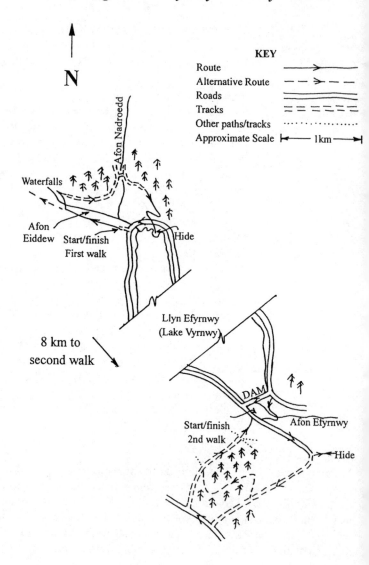

N

KEY

Route	
Alternative Route	
Roads	
Tracks	
Other paths/tracks	
Approximate Scale	⊢—— 1km ——⊣

Afon Nadroedd

Waterfalls

Afon
Eiddew

Start/finish
First walk

Hide

Llyn Efyrnwy
(Lake Vyrnwy)

8 km to
second walk

DAM

Start/finish
2nd walk

Afon Efyrnwy

Hide

These are some of the most impressive falls in the Berwyn: although not as high as those in Pistyll Rhaeadr, they carry a much greater volume of water (very peaty). They are magnificent at any time, but particularly so after heavy rain. They fall about one hundred metres in a series of large steps, in a distance of less than two hundred metres.

For a close examination of the falls, you can follow a path on their left hand side, but our route goes back for about 100 metres to a wooden foot bridge on your left (north).

[**Alternative longer route:** You can continue up alongside the falls, and out on to the moors. You need to be prepared to get your feet wet, and it is necessary to cross a couple of fences without the benefit of stiles. You may have to walk quite a long way before you can cross the river, but this is usually possible on an S bend, where there is an island in the middle, with a couple of small jumps or large strides. This is about half a kilometre after you have passed the ruins of Blaen-y-coed on the far bank. You can head north-west from here to the summit of Bwlan (528 metres), but this is not a very exciting hill. However, you get good views to the west and north of the south-western Berwyn summits. For the Berwyn, there is remarkably little heather, and walking is not too tough. Descend south to Blaen-y-coed. The ruins are quite extensive and obviously the area has not been used for a long time, since many of the remains are grass covered. Follow the path (often very faint) south-east from Blaen-y-coed, high above the falls (on your right) and with excellent views, back to the forest and then descend very steeply to your right (south-west) alongside the forest fence to rejoin the original route just below the falls. This adds about 5 kilometres distance, and 300 metres ascent, to the walk]

2. Cross the bridge, turn left alongside the forest, and you reach the bottom of the falls on the opposite side in a short distance. Those with nimble feet can reach the same place by using the stepping stones from the far side of the falls. Having finished looking at the falls, turn round and walk back towards the forest, but now stay on the main track that runs down the left hand side. You disappear into the forest and after about a kilometre the track turns left and you descend gently in a northerly direction. The track is way marked with green arrows. After

a few hundred metres you meet a rickety bridge on the right which you cross, and again turn right, back down the far side of the river (Afon Nadroedd). You follow the path around and down through the forest, and it takes on the appearance of an ancient track because across the gently slopping hillside, there is a horizontal section about three or four metres wide which, although not well trodden today, has a row of very ancient trees along its right hand side. Leave the forest and turn right down a small track which leads, inside a couple of hundred metres, back to the road. Cross the road almost immediately, and follow the signs to the RSPB Hide, which is only about 200 metres down this track.

The hide is ideally placed for looking at the birds on the water just in front of you, and there are plenty of illustrations indicating the kind of birds you are likely to see. However, whether you happen to see them or not is quite a matter of chance and the time of year.

Retrace your steps from the hide back to the road, and turn left. After half a kilometre you will arrive back at the car park. This may be a good opportunity to eat lunch in the picnic area.

3. To reach the second walk, you have to drive 5 miles down the south side of Lake Vyrnwy. Drive straight past the dam and after about half a kilometre, almost at the end of the road, there are several car parks. The one down a short road on your left (the Village car park) is convenient for the walk. Walk back up to the dam, and turn right to walk along the top of it.

There are several signs giving you information about the dam which was completed in 1891 and flooded the village of Llanwddyn in the process. Looking out across Lake Vyrnwy, which is Severn Trent Water's largest reservoir, you can see to your right the Gothic Tower, where water leaves the reservoir on its way to the inhabitants of Liverpool.

Continue across the dam and turn right at the end of it. Almost immediately, there is a way mark path on your right dropping down below the dam into the valley. In the valley you cross a dry river bed, where the river was diverted whilst the dam was being built. Continue along the pleasant way marked path, past a weir on the river, until eventually you come to a footbridge, and you turn right across it. Once across, turn right and shortly, right again off the road onto a path through the trees alongside the river. You now pass the weir on the far bank, and then turn left away from the river soon returning to the car park.

4. Continue up through the car park to the road and then turn left, and soon you will find a blue way marked trail called the Craig Garth-bwlch Trail. You walk gently up hill on a minor road (initially metalled), and soon leave the woods. At the top of the hill, about a kilometre from the car park, and on a sharp right hand bend, there is a small track leading you off left to the bird hide.

The bird hide overlooks the hillside and there are a variety of woodland birds, indicated on posters in the hide, that you might see here, but of course that cannot be guaranteed. However what is certain, weather permitting, is that the view in the opposite direction from the hide, down across Lake Vyrnwy, is excellent and probably one of the best views of the dam and the lake.

5. Return from the bird hide back to the road, and continue to follow it. It carries on gently up hill for quite some time, and then starts to drop through the woods.

[**Alternative more strenuous route:** If you wish to get a good view of the valley on your left, look out for red way marked signs – you will find the first one on your right about a kilometre from the hide. You go very steeply up through the forest. At the top of the steep section, you turn left and continue along the track, which goes gently up and down, some way below the summit. Eventually you emerge from the forest and get excellent views over the valley to your left (south). From here, the signs are quite confusing and appear to send you down a track on your right – do not go this way, the track ends in the middle of nowhere. Instead, continue along the original track which bears right after a few metres, and descends to rejoin the original blue way marked track at a T junction, where you turn right]

You reach a road about 1.5 kilometres from the hide, and turn right; after about 200 metres, look out for way marked paths back through the forest on your right, and follow them. Going through the forest there are a couple of options, but they lead to the same place. After about a kilometre, you come to a five-way junction at the edge of the forest. You take the minor way marked path down hill (north-east) and get a good view of the dam and lake as you descend towards the car park, which is less than a kilometre away.

Cwm Hirnant and the far western Berwyn Mountains

OS Maps:	1:50,000 Landranger 125, Bala and Lake Vyrnwy
	1:25,000 Pathfinder 825, Bala
Start and finish:	Cwm Hirnant, near Bwlch yr Hwch
Access:	About 2 kilometres (1.5 miles) south of Bala on the B4391, turn right (signed Rhos-y-gwaliau) and follow this road (which becomes single track) for about 9 kilometres (5 miles). There is no public transport.
Parking:	300 metres past a bridge as you leave the forested area, where upper cwm comes into view, there is a small car park on the right hand side (GR952296)
Grade:	Moderate, mostly on reasonable paths or tracks, but there are some pathless sections to contend with.
Height gain	About 450 metres
Facilities:	None
Overview:	This is a beautiful circular walk around the remote Cwm Hirnant, with tremendous views to the west.

Walk Directions:

1. From the car park go west directly up the hill, aiming for the left hand side of the wood in front of you. After a few hundred metres, you reach a fence, which you must cross. There is no stile, take care not to injure yourself or damage the fence. Continue on the left hand side of another fence up the hillside. The hillside is very steep initially but the gradient eases after about three quarters of a kilometre, and you have done the bulk of the day's climbing. When you reach the high point of the ridge turn left (south), and try to find yourself a handy sheep track

Walk Nine - Cwm Hirnant: the far Western Berwyn Mountains

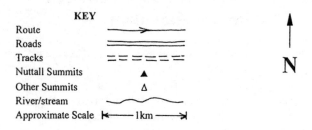

KEY

Route	
Roads	
Tracks	
Nuttall Summits	▲
Other Summits	Δ
River/stream	
Approximate Scale	⊢——1km——⊣

N

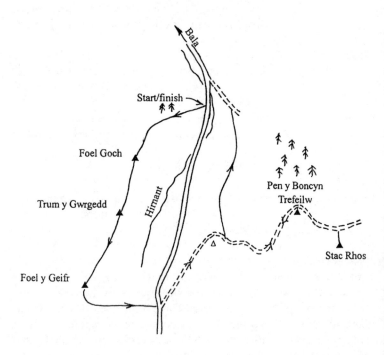

Bala

Start/finish

Foel Goch

Hirnant

Trum y Gwrgedd

Pen y Boncyn
Trefeilw

Δ

Foel y Geifr

Stac Rhos

to the summit of Foel Goch. There are not many around here, and the heather starts to pull at the ankles, but only for a short distance. When you reach the summit of Foel Goch, which is marked by the smallest of cairns, take a breather and have a look at the spectacular views.

The most impressive feature of the sky line is the Aran Mountains, which are south-west of where you stand. They are very dramatic from this spot. As you scan towards the north, you see the Rhinogau on the horizon, then the Arenig and finally the Snowdon massif in the far distance. To the south, you can make out the trig point on Foel y Geifr. Looking east, the view is totally different because now you look out over the main Berwyn plateau. From here the main peaks of Cadair Berwyn, Cadair Bronwen and Moel Sych are mere bumps on the horizon, because you cannot see the steep eastern escarpment. In the north east, the Clwydian hills fade away into the distance. All in all, beautiful views.

From Foel Goch you follow the broad ridge towards Trum y Gwrgedd, and if you search around you will find some reasonable animal tracks to follow. Within a few hundred metres you cross Trum y Gwrgedd, your second Nuttall of the day. From here it is about one kilometre to Foel y Geifr, and at times the track is quite boggy. If you are really lucky you may find a track right to the trig point on the summit, but most times when I have been there, the last couple of hundred metres are walked in knee deep heather.

2. From here you turn your back on the glorious views to the west and head due east to the top of the cwm. There is definitely no path here, but it is easy to pick your way through the heather on grass. The going is not too tough and you reach the road in just under a kilometre. From here you pick up a land rover track heading north-east, which is presumably used for forestry activities. You walk steadily up hill for a kilometre, where you reach the high point of the track.

[**Alternative longer route:** It is quite easy from here to pick up another couple of Nuttalls, Pen y Boncyn Trefeilw and Stac Rhos. You continue along the track, initially in an easterly direction reaching the former inside a kilometre, and the latter a further half kilometre on. In each case, the summits are just off the track to the right. Including the return, this adds about three kilometres distance, and about 100 metres of ascent]

Along this track you get a great feeling of spaciousness, and it feels very remote. Despite the fact that you are on a good track, you are unlikely to meet anyone at all. It is a very peaceful place – the haunt of buzzard and hen harrier, and in the summer it has the permanent song of sky larks which do not appear to be in decline hereabouts. Unlike many of the walks in this guide, apart from the land rover track and some forestry, there is little to indicate man's presence – and what exists is not particularly desirable. However, the track is preferable to heather bashing, even if it is a bit of an eye sore.

3. Here we turn left (north) down a hill on a well marked track. However, after about 600 metres, the track finishes at a gate into a field. You pass through this gate and walk more or less down the centre of the field and after another few hundred metres, you meet another fence and there is a gate in the centre of this. You continue down the next field, and in the bottom right hand corner there is another gate and the track magically reappears. You follow this down to the next fence where once again it disappears. Go through the gate and turn right. Almost immediately there is a small stile. Cross this, just above a small pond (surrounded by greater reed mace or bulrushes); cross the bridge to join a main track coming in from your right. Within a hundred metres or so you will be back at the road bridge you crossed earlier in the day and on your way to the car park. Turn left up the road, and it is just a gentle walk of a few hundred metres back to your car.

Cadair Bronwen, Cadair Berwyn and Moel Sych from Llandrillo

OS Maps:	1:50,000 Landranger 125, Bala and Lake Vyrnwy.
	1:25,000 Pathfinder 826, Llandrillo.
Start and finish:	Llandrillo
Access:	Llandrillo is a village in the Dee Valley between Corwen and Bala. It is approximately 8 kilometres (5 miles) south-west of Corwen, on the B4401.
Parking:	There is a small car park on the riverside, towards the eastern end of the village (GR 035372).
Grade:	Strenuous, but mostly on reasonable paths.
Height gain	About 900 metres.
Facilities:	The village has a Post Office/ General Stores, and a licensed restaurant. There is a small picnic area and toilets in the car park. There are no facilities on route.
Overview:	This circular walk includes the 3 major peaks of the Berwyn, but can be easily modified to reach either Cadair Bronwen or Cadair Berwyn on their own, or any two from three. These shorter routes do not significantly reduce the grade. The walk also includes a visit to the Stone Circle at Moel Ty-uchaf.

Walk Directions:

1. From the car park, turn left onto the B4401 towards Corwen. After 50 metres, bear right at the church onto a minor road and follow it eastwards. It soon starts to climb, and after about a kilometre, you pass through a gate into a mixed woodland. The track is no longer metalled

Walk Ten - Cadair Bronwen, Cadair Berwyn and Moel Sych from Llandrillo

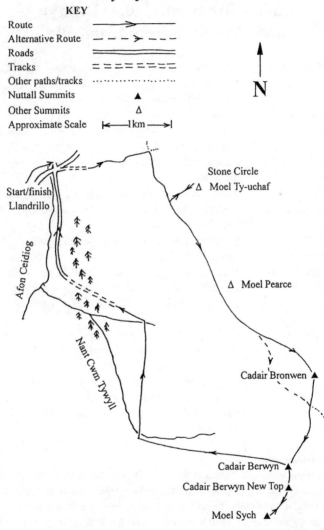

KEY

Route	→
Alternative Route	– – → – –
Roads	═══
Tracks	═ ═ ═ ═ ═
Other paths/tracks	··········
Nuttall Summits	▲
Other Summits	△
Approximate Scale	⊢—1km—⊣

N

Stone Circle
△ Moel Ty-uchaf

Start/finish
Llandrillo

Afon Ceidiog

△ Moel Pearce

Nant Cwm Tywyll

Cadair Bronwen ▲

Cadair Berwyn ▲
Cadair Berwyn New Top ▲
Moel Sych ▲

as it follows the left hand side of the wood in a north-easterly direction. You continue to gain height, and there are occasionally good views through the trees of the Dee Valley and the Arenig Mountains. You leave the wood and continue to climb gently along the side of a wall, until you reach another mixed woodland. Here you cross a stream and follow the wood's south-east boundary to another ford, on the far side of the wood, after about 200 metres. The path now bends right and continues almost due east, still alongside the wall, and after about 350 metres you meet a major track, just before a small wood. At this junction you turn right (south). The summit of Moel Ty-uchaf (440 metres) is now in front of you to the left, and the track passes it by on the right. To visit the stone circle, you can either, after passing through a gate about 300 metres passed the junction, aim directly for the summit of Moel Ty-uchaf, or continue along the track for a further 400 metres by which time the circle will be clearly visible, about 150 metres away on your left, near the summit.

Although quite small, this is an excellent stone circle. The stones are not high but are closely spaced, and in the centre there is a small depression, presumably the remains of a burial cyst. The views from here are splendid. You can see Cadair Bronwen, with its large summit cairn, just over three kilometres to the south-east; to the west, you can see the Snowdon massif and many other Welsh mountains to the south of it.

2. You return to the track and continue, still gently climbing, towards Cadair Bronwen. Moel Pearce is bypassed on its right (south) side after about 1600 metres and about 800 metres later, near Trawsnant, there is a cairn on the left of the track.

The cairn is surmounted by a small slab with an inscription "Carnedd John Fronllan, Llangwn 1891". At least I think that's what it says but it's not too clear. I wonder who John Fronllan was? Shortly beyond this point you can see all of the main Berwyn Summits in front of you – Cadair Bronwen, Cadair Berwyn, Cadair Berwyn New Top and Moel Sych from left to right.

Shortly after this the main track bears right towards Bwlch Maen Gwynedd, the pass between Cadair Bronwen and Cadair Berwyn, but you take the left hand branch and follow the fence aiming directly towards the summit of Cadair Bronwen. Until now the paths have been good, but this path soon deteriorates; it is often barely discernible and the area close to the fence can be very boggy. You reach the summit of Cadair Bronwen (785 metres) with its enormous summit cairn (called Bwrdd Arthur, Arthur's Table) after about 800 metres.

The views are very rewarding and this is the only one of the major summits from which Bala Lake can be seen, The main Berwyn ridge with its impressive eastern escarpment stretches to the south; the Snowdon Massif is in the distance to the west; and we can identify the Arenig, Aran, Rhinog ranges, and many of the other summits in Snowdonia. To the north you can see the most northerly Berwyn mountain; Moel Fferna and the other Berwyn summits fade away to the south and south-west. If you search around the summit you may well find the cloudberry. This blackberry like plant has sharp tasting orange berries, and this is the only place in Wales where it is found which is reflected in its Welsh name, mwyar Berwyn.

3. You now descend south towards Bwlch Maen Gwynedd which you reach after about 600 metres.

This pass is on an ancient hill track, said to be Roman, called Ffordd Gam Elin. The track goes from just North of Llandrillo to Llanrhaeadr-ym-Mochnant and is in fact the route you were following passed the stone circle. The track name means Helen's crooked road, and Helen is believed to have been a Welsh princess who was married to a Roman Emperor.

If you are only intent on visiting Cadair Bronwen, turn right (west) onto Ffordd Gam Elin at the bwlch, soon rejoining the route you originally followed from Llandrillo. However if you plan to visit Cadair Berwyn and Moel Sych, you continue south up hill, initially steep and often boggy, until you reach the summit of Cadair Berwyn in a little over a kilometre. Although there is a trig point here, it is not the highest point, which is a further 300 metres on and is called Cadair Berwyn New Top.

Looking east from here, there is a splendid view of Cwm Maen Gwynedd. The eastern escarpment drops very sharply to the valley floor, 200 metres below and the minor Nuttalls along the sides of the horseshoe are clearly visible. In the distance, you can see some English high ground.

4. From here it is only a few hundred metres in a south westerly direction to the summit of Moel Sych. To return to Llandrillo you walk back to the triangulation point on Cadair Berwyn and here there is a sign to Llandrillo pointing westerly across the moors. There is no real path until, after a few hundred metres, you begin to descend Foel Fawr. The path, which looks as though it was made by a four wheeled vehicle, often contains water when it has been raining. About two kilometres from the summit of Cadair Berwyn, there is a minor summit. Continue over it and down the broad ridge, a little north of west. In a little less than a kilometre, there are signs of quarrying activity about 50 metres to the left of the path, and about 50 metres further on, the remains of a ruined circular building. The latter is about 5 metres in diameter and still 1.5 metres high in places. Shortly after this there is a broad saddle and the land then begins to rise gently in a broad ridge swinging toward the north-west. There is a faint track across this ridge but this is not the correct way. Following it would lead on to Nyrs Gron and Cadwst which would interfere with farming activities.

5. Instead, follow a way marked path in a northerly direction. The first way mark is not easy to see from the path. To find it, look out for a marshy area just before the saddle. Turn right here (north) leaving the faint path and aim for a ruined building about 100 metres away. Just before the ruin, there is a way marked stile. Cross this and, a few metres later, Nant Cwm Tywyll. Continue in a northerly direction, following one of the many sheep tracks that contour along the hillside, to another way marked stile which is reached after five or six hundred metres. Cross this and a short section of very boggy ground: the path now continues, still generally northerly, to the right of a fence which eventually becomes a stone wall before meeting yet another way marked stile after about 800 metres. After Crossing this and Clochnant (via stepping stones), turn left (westerly) and the faint path you have been following for the last several kilometres soon becomes more substantial. By the time you reach the boundary of the Berwyn National Nature Reserve, about 200 metres further on, it becomes an unmade road. Continue down the road, which soon becomes metalled, to reach Llandrillo after a little more than 2 kilometres.

The Berwyn Nuttalls – the North-East Group from Moel Fferna to Post Gwyn

OS Maps:	1:50,000 Landranger 125, Bala and Lake Vyrnwy 1:25,00 Pathfinder 805 Corwen, 826 Llandrillo and 846, Tanat Valley
Start:	Llidiart y Parc
Access:	Llidiart y Parc is on the A5, about three kilometres (two miles) east of Corwen, and ten kilometres (six miles) west of Llangollen
Parking:	Although there is limited parking on verges in the centre of Llidiart (GR 119434), mostly used by locals, a better option is to use a large lay by on the south side of the A5, a few hundred metres towards Corwen
Finish:	Tanypistyll
Access:	From the centre of Llanrhaeadr-ym-Mochnant, follow the minor single track road (signed Waterfall Rhaeadr) on the north side of Afon Rhaeadr to the end – approximately seven kilometres (four miles)
Parking:	There are two small free parking areas on the left hand side, about 100 metres from the end of the road; or there is a pay car park (modest charge) at the end of the road (GR 074295).
Grade:	Strenuous
Height gain	About 1800 metres
Facilities:	Llidiart y Parc has a garage/general stores; a public house (500 metres away on the Carrog road) which serves food; and a small campsite next to the railway station, with very limited facilities.
	Tanypistyll has toilets, a telephone and a small café. The latter is not always open in the winter.

Walk Eleven - The North-East Berwyn Mountains

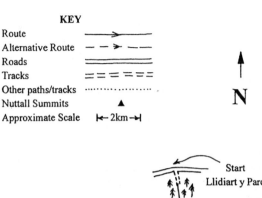

KEY

Route	
Alternative Route	
Roads	
Tracks	
Other paths/tracks	
Nuttall Summits	▲
Approximate Scale	⊢ 2km ⊣

N

Start
Llidiart y Parc

1 Moel Fferna
2 Pen Bwlch Llandrillo Top
3 Cadair Bronwen NE Top
4 Cadair Bronwen
5 Tomle
6 Foel Wen
7 Foel Wen South Top
8 Mynydd Tarw
9 Godor
10 Godor North Top
11 Moel Yr Ewig
12 Cadair Berwyn
13 Cadair Berwyn New Top
14 Moel Sych
15 Post Gwyn

Maiden's Path

Tyn-y-ffridd

Finish
Tan y pistyll

	There is also a small family campsite with limited facilities
Overview:	This is a demanding walk, for fit people only, which takes in fifteen of the Berwyn Nuttalls. It is not convenient to do this as a circular walk, and transport therefore is required at the end of the walk, where public transport is non-existent. The paths are mostly quite good though often boggy, and only occasionally are excursions into the heather required.

Walk Directions:

These route directions are brief and confined to route finding only, since I believe anyone undertaking this type of walk will not find too much time to admire the scenery in detail.

1. Follow the minor road south from the centre of Llidiart y Parc, opposite the phone box, and walk up into the forest. There are many tracks through the forest and it is difficult to decide which is the shortest, but eventually you will leave the forest after about 1.5 kilometres. Now you need to find the track going up across the moor, still in a southerly direction. For a while this track is quite good, but you need to find a minor path heading off right towards Moel Fferna. This minor path, which is quite difficult to find, is about a kilometre after the forest ends, and starts near the point where you cross the saddle of the south-easterly tongue running down from Moel Fferna. You now head south-west to the summit of Moel Fferna. If you fail to find this minor track, it is hard going through the heather to the summit.

2. From the summit, which has no trig point although the map does, you go south-easterly for a while along a minor track, until you meet a fence going more or less east-west. You cross the fence here *via* a stile, and head south-west following the right hand side of another fence. The path is reasonable, though often boggy. You cross Cerrig Coediog and a few other minor summits, and after about four kilometres you reach your second Nuttall of the day, Pen Bwlch Llandrillo Top. This summit is poorly defined, but it does have a reasonable cairn. Retrace your steps from the summit for about 100

metres, back to a stile in the fence. Cross this, head due south and in a very short time you reach the Maidens' path at the Wayfarer's memorial. You cross the track, heading south, and after about 1.5 kilometres you reach Cadair Bronwen North-East Top. From here, your third Nuttall, it is about a kilometre uphill to Cadair Bronwen your fourth Nuttall. You descend steeply south to Bwlch Maen Gwynedd, and turn left onto an ancient trackway, Ffordd Gam Elin, which continues on to a boundary stone.

3.   Here you leave the path, which goes down into the valley, and head east crossing the next Nuttall, Tomle; then Foel Wen, your sixth Nuttall. You head south-east to cross the seventh Nuttall, Foel Wen South Top; and on to the eighth Nuttall, Mynydd Tarw. From here there is quite a big descent alongside the forest, and then onto a track leading down to Tyn-y-ffridd.

4.   You cross the road and shortly bear west and climb up to Godor, the ninth Nuttall. Now once more on the ridge, make sure that you keep to the faint paths about here, because the heather can be fierce.

Continue over Godor North Top, the tenth Nuttall; and Moel Yr Ewig, the eleventh Nuttall. As you approach the steep eastern escarpment of the main Berwyn ridge, aim north-west between Cadair Berwyn and Cadair Berwyn New Top; although there is no path, it is not too difficult to scramble up here (If you feel uncomfortable about scrambling steeply up a loose slope without the benefit of a path, aim south-west where there is a path that will bring you to the ridge between Moel Sych and Cadair Berwyn New Top). When you meet the ridge, you go north for a few hundred metres to bag Cadair Berwyn (Nuttall number 12) and then turn round and retrace your steps for a couple of hundred metres. Then continue south along the ridge to Cadair Berwyn New Top, your thirteenth Nuttall – two to go! From Cadair Berwyn New Top, it is just a short descent followed by a short climb to Moel Sych – Nuttall number 14.

5. From Moel Sych you head west down hill, and after about a kilometre, where the fence does an acute left hand turn, you leave the path and go half left (south-west) down into the valley. There is no real path but the going is fair and if visibility is good, aim just right of Post Gwyn, the highest point on the ridge across the valley in front of you. Almost at the bottom of the valley, you cross a small double stream

and if you are lucky, pick up an animal track which leads to the small river (Afon Disgynfa), which you cross, in a couple of hundred metres. You should be slightly west of Post Gwyn's summit because here, after leaving the marshy area around the river, you will find an easy heather free passage to the ridge a few hundred metres west of Post Gwyn. Turn left (east) to reach the summit of Post Gwyn, the fifteenth Nuttall, in a few minutes.

6. From here you continue in an easterly direction, initially staying to the left (north) of the ridge to find the easiest ground, until you reach Cwm-yr-ast. Near the top of the cwm, you meet a path going north-east towards Craig-y-mwn and arrive at the latter where a stream (Nantygaseg) charges over the cliff. You pass through a gap in the fence to your left, to find a faint exposed path going south-east downwards across the face of a steep slope. At the bottom, turn left and you will soon arrive in Tanypistyll (see walk 5).

The Berwyn Nuttalls – the South-West Group from Foel Cwm-Sian Llwyd to Foel Goch

OS Maps:	1:50,000 Landranger 125, Bala and Lake Vyrnwy
	1:25,000 Pathfinder 826, Bala
Start:	Milltir Gerrig
Access:	Milltir Gerrig is on the B4391, approximately five kilometres (three miles) north-west of Llangynog, and may be approached either from Bala, about 40 kilometres (25 miles); or Corwen, about 21 kilometres (13 miles).
Parking:	There is ample parking space at Milltir Gerrig (GR 018303)
Finishing Point	A small car park below Foel Goch (Grid reference 952296) in Cwm Hirnant, on the unclassified road running from Bala Lake to Lake Vyrnwy (see walk 9).
Parking:	There is space for several cars
Grade:	Strenuous
Height gain	About 700 metres
Facilities:	None, and there is no public transport to the start or finish of this walk
Overview:	Despite being only about 16 kilometres, and with relatively modest ascent (700 metres), this is a tough walk which takes in 9 Nuttalls. The heather is particularly tough, and there are many stretches where there are no paths.

Walk Directions:

These route directions are brief and confined to route finding only, since I believe anyone undertaking this type of walk will not find too much time to admire the scenery in detail.

1. From Milltir Gerrig, go down the road towards Llangynog for about 200 metres, and then turn right on to a track. After a further 200

Walk Twelve - The South-West Berwyn Mountains

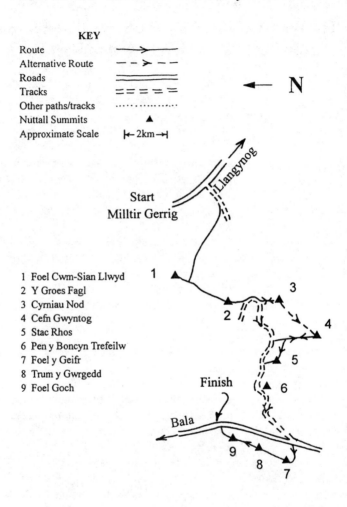

KEY

Route	
Alternative Route	
Roads	
Tracks	
Other paths/tracks	
Nuttall Summits	▲
Approximate Scale	⊢— 2km —⊣

N

Start
Milltir Gerrig

Llangynog

1 Foel Cwm-Sian Llwyd
2 Y Groes Fagl
3 Cyrniau Nod
4 Cefn Gwyntog
5 Stac Rhos
6 Pen y Boncyn Trefeilw
7 Foel y Geifr
8 Trum y Gwrgedd
9 Foel Goch

Finish

Bala

metres, you ford a small stream and immediately turn right, next to a clump of conifers. Go up the steep bank and then follow a good track, initially alongside a fence, heading towards Foel Cwm-Siân Llwyd. The path is quite good for a kilometre or so, until you reach a stile which you cross to a small marsh. Now the going gets tough and the heather begins in earnest; it is very hard to find a path, but within a few hundred metres you reach the ridge and turn right to reach Foel Cwm-Siân Llwyd, your first Nuttall, in about 150 metres.

2. Retrace your steps south along the ridge across Trum y Sarn and continue on to Y Groes Fagl – the second Nuttall of this route. This is approximately 2.5 kilometres from Foel Cwm-Siân Llwyd: initially the path is reasonable but becomes very faint, and the last few hundred metres to the summit – which is marked by a two metre post – is hard work on a peaty path. Shortly after Y Groes Fagl, you reach a Land Rover track which you follow south through the bwlch; but the relief is short lived and when the track swings west, you leave it and continue south. The going is initially tough and boggy, but you meet a fence about 300 metres before the summit of Cyrniau Nod (the 3rd Nuttall), alongside of which there is a reasonable path. This summit is marked by a large cairn and is about 600 metres from the Land Rover track. Now you retrace your steps back to the Land Rover track, and follow it in a westerly direction for a kilometre or so, passing over Foel Cedig until you are due north of Cefn Gwyntog. The heather is unavoidable now as you head south, crossing a fence with a boundary stone after 200 metres, to reach the summit of Cefn Gwyntog, your 4th Nuttall after about a kilometre. Retrace your steps through the heather to the boundary stone, and turn left (west) alongside it, where the going is mostly good though sometimes boggy, for about 500-600 metres; the summit of Stac Rhos (Nuttall number 5) is just to your right (north), and not easy to identify.

[**Alternative shorter route**: Instead of going back to the Land Rover track from Cyrniau Nod, you can go cross country to Cefn Gwyntog: this saves a least 2 kilometres, at the expense of much harder going. From Cyrniau Nod, head south-west to pick up Nant Cyrniau Nod – follow the course of this stream, as near as is practicable, to the summit of Cefn Gwyntog: following the stream minimises the amount of heather, but it is still a tough leg of about 1.5 kilometres. From here, follow the route described above to Stac Rhos.]

3. From Stac Rhos, head north to reach the Land Rover track in a few hundred metres of delightfully easy going grass. Follow the track round, again westerly, to Pen y Boncyn Trefeilw (Nuttall Number 6) the summit of which is 50 metres or so to the south of the track, on a fence at a boundary stone. The Land Rover track now continues southerly for a while and then you climb gently in a westerly direction to near the summit of Pen y Cerrig Duon. Here the track turns almost south, and in just over a kilometre you reach the highest point of Cwm Hirnant on the minor unclassified road running between Bala and Lake Vyrnwy.

4. The seventh Nuttall, Foel y Geifr is directly to your west and there is no path, but if you aim slightly to the left of the summit, you can miss the worst of the heather. From the summit, which is only about a kilometre from the road, you now head north-east to Trum y Gwrgedd, Nuttall Number 8. Keep your eyes open, because there is a narrow track which runs all the way along this ridge, crossing Trum Y Gwrgedd, and then continuing on to Foel Goch, the 9th and final Nuttall on this route. From Foel Goch the path disappears, but you continue along the ridge until you reach the fence. Turn right at the fence and follow it steeply down hill to the edge of the forest, and then continue down to the car park.

[**Alternative longer route:** To make this a real marathon effort, you can continue on to Moel y Cerrig Duon. If you plan to do this from the road at the top of Cwm Hirnant, it is best to take a diagonal approach to pick up Trum y Gwrgedd, leave your bag there, and then walk north to Foel Goch. Retrace your steps to Trum y Gwrgedd, pick up your bag and then head south-west to Foel y Geifr. From here you have got several kilometres of really rough going, but stick to the high ground as much as possible, initially aiming south-west to Cefn Coch, and then south to Moel y Cerrig Duon. Moel y Cerrig Duon is officially classified as an Aran Nuttall, but it is on the same high ground as the Berwyn Nuttalls you have just crossed, and also to the west of Cwm Cynllwyd which may be taken as the natural divider between the Aran and the Berwyn mountains. From Moel y Cerrig Duon the best ending point would be to walk on south-westerly to the car park at Bwlch y Groes. You have now extended the walk by four or five kilometres, and although the ascent has not increased a great deal, the going is very rough and it is a very tough event.]

APPENDIX A: THE BERWYN NUTTALLS

NAME	GRID REF	SPOT HEIGHT Metres
Moel Fferna	117398	630
Pen Bwlch Llandrillo Top	090369	621
Cadair Bronwen North East Top	087352	700
Cadair Bronwen	077346	785
Tomle	085335	742
Foel Wen	099334	691
Foel Wen South Top	103330	687
Mynydd Tarw	113324	681
Godor	095307	679
Godor North Top	089311	675
Moel yr Ewig	081318	698
Cadair Berwyn	072327	827
Cadair Berwyn New Top	072324	830
Moel Sych	066318	827
Post Gwyn	049294	665
Foel Cwm-Siân Llwyd	996314	648
Y Groes Fagl	988290	659
Cyrniau Nod	989279	667
Cefn Gwyntog	976266	615
Stac Rhos	969279	630
Pen y Boncyn Trefeilw	963283	646
Foel y Geifr	937275	626
Trum y Gwragedd	942284	612
Foel Goch	943291	613

APPENDIX B: THE BERWYN NUTTALS LINK

This route links walks eleven and twelve allowing 24 (or possibly 25) Nuttalls to be completed at one time. This is a very demanding event and 16 hours would be a very good time for its completion.

From Post Gwyn (walk 11) follow the broad ridge north west. The path is at best faint, often boggy and sometimes difficult to follow but it is mostly down hill. The ridge converges with the main ridge from Moel Sych, running down towards Milltir Gerrig after about two kilometres. The last 200 metres are almost due north through powerful Berwyn heather. You have now reached the main Moel Sych to Milltir Gerrig path, which is good though often boggy but nearer to the road there are a lot of duck boards. Milltir Gerrig is reached after about 3.5 kilometres from the summit of Post Gwyn, and this is where you start walk 12.

APPENDIX C: SOME COMMON WELSH WORDS USED IN PLACE NAMES AND TOPOGRAPHICAL FEATURES

The following list will help you translate some Welsh place names which I think helps enjoyment of the walks. It is also useful because the place names give you an indication of what you might find or see. For example, Blaen-y-cwm means head of the valley and Rhosybeddau means moor of the graves.

Afon	River
Allt	Wood or Hill
Bach/Fach	Little
Bedd/Beddau	Grave/Graves
Blaen	Head (of valley)
Bwlch	Pass
Cadair	Seat
Caer	Fort
Coch	Red
Coed	Wood

Craig	Rock or Crag
Cwm	Valley
Du, Ddu	Black
Dyffryn	Valley
Fford	Road
Ffridd	Mountain Pasture
Gwyn	White
Hirnant	Long Stream
Llan	Church
Llwybr	Path
Llwyd	Grey
Llyn	Lake
Maen	Rock
Mawr/Fawr	Big
Moel	Bare Hill
Mynydd	Mountain
Nant	Stream
Parc	Field/Park
Pen	Head
Pistyll	Spring
Pont	Bridge
Rhaeadr	Waterfall
Rhiw	Hill
Rhos	Moor
Sych	Dry
Tarw	Bull
Trum	Ridge/Crest
Ty'n (Tyddyn)	Small Farm